EUROPA MILITARIA

SPECIAL Nº9

GERMAN NAPOLEONIC ARMIES

RECREATED IN COLOUR PHOTOGRAPHS

TORSTEN VERHÜLSDONK
& CARL SCHULZE

Windrow & Greene

© 1996 Windrow & Greene Ltd

This edition published
in Great Britain 1996 by
Windrow & Greene Ltd
5 Gerrard Street
London W1V 7LJ

Designed by John Anastasio/Creative Line
Printed in Spain

A CIP catalogue record for this book is
available from the British Library.

ISBN 1 85915 092 6

Acknowledgements
The authors would like to express their thanks
to the re-enactment groups, and to their individual
members, whose patient assistance made these
photographs possible. They fulfilled all our
wishes regarding their posing, and answered our
endless questions, down to the contents of the
smallest pocket. We would also like to thank
Petra Linke for her help in forming rational
sentences out of our sometimes confused train of thoughts.

CONTENTS

PREFACE & FOREWORD

About ten years ago, when the hobby of Napoleonic re-enactment had its cautious beginnings on the Continent, no one could have imagined that the 180th anniversary of Waterloo in 1995 would see 5,000 participants on the battlefield.

The Napoleonische Gesellschaft (the German counterpart to the British-based Napoleonic Association, to which most of the groups featured in this book belong) has developed into an authoritative institution of historical reconstruction, thanks to the dedication of many of its members. Intensive and meticulous research has combined with the never-ending practical effort to improve the equipment and appearance of the uniformed groups.

A positive impulse was given by the fall of the Iron Curtain, enabling many Eastern groups to get in contact at last with their Western counterparts, to the enrichment of both; today groups from the Czech Republic, Russia and Lithuania often march in our ranks. Thanks to the active groups based around Leipzig and Jena these historic sites are now properly respected, and re-enactors enjoy access to the battlefields.

Quality and professionalism in appearance, drill and weapons handling are nowadays the foundation of serious military history displays; but the appeal of this hobby extends beyond the "drill book" aspects, satisfying though they are. The sight of a good re-enactment unit off-duty can sometimes give a convincing glimpse into history: in their camps the soldiers sleep on straw, cook at campfires with contemporary-style pots and pans, while away their time cleaning their metal equipment with brick-powder, playing contemporary card games, and singing the songs of the Napoleonic period. Those who put their hearts into the hobby can disappear into the past for two or three days.

In the beginning most groups focussed their interest on the end of this era, and the battle of Waterloo where victory finally crowned the German campaigns of liberation, 1813-15. Today re-enactors apply themselves to the whole scope of the Napoleonic Wars, especially in anniversary years; events marking these began with the bicentennial of Valmy in 1992, continued with the anniversaries of the campaigns on the Rhine and in Belgium to reach Italy in 1996, commemorating the rising star of Bonaparte. The years to come will see re-enacted engagements on many battlefields of this, one of the most important periods of European history. Our members will save these sites from oblivion, and fill them with new life.

This book, in its German edition, is intended to encourage interest in our activities, but also to serve as a guide for costume designers, painters or figure modellers. An important aspect of the living history hobby, beyond the actual historical displays, is the opportunity it gives for contact and co-operation with our friends from all over

At Plancenoit, near the Prussian memorial to the dead of Waterloo, a skirmish was fought during the 1995 re-enactment. Afterwards an act of commemoration was held for the fallen of both sides; and the Prussian groups presented arms as the "enemy" marched off - only a small gesture, but typical of re-enactors, who are united by their understanding that the suffering of the rank-and-file was the same in all historical armies.

Europe. Through this bloodless re-creation of a multinational "Grande Armée" personal friendships develop across national borders, deepening our hope that none of the European nations will ever again face each other under arms.

I would like to thank here all those who have contributed so much time, energy and goodwill to the development of our hobby, and to the many collectors and museums who have provided the sources for uniforms and equipment.

Finally, one man in particular should be mentioned whose ideals were very much those expressed in the lines

(**Above**) Prussian infantry of the Line and Landwehr units fought side by side against the French in the Wars of Liberation, and in 1815 together with British, Dutch Belgian, Nassau and Hanoverian forces in the final campaign of the 20-year Napoleonic Wars.

above. Friedrich Bauer served as chairman of the Napoleonische Gesellschaft for several years; his untimely death has left a serious gap in our ranks, and this book should be dedicated to his memory.

Alfred Umhey
President,
Napoleonische Gesellschaft

*   *   *

The hobby of re-enactment or "living history" embraces a huge range of historical periods: Romans, Vikings, Normans, High Medieval, English Civil War, 18th Century, Napoleonic, American Civil War, and both World Wars. Each period has its enthusiastic followers and its special attractions; what they share is the hunger not just to learn about history from written sources, but to feel it.

Re-enactment means a lot more than just dressing up in a colourful uniform. Real re-enactors are also "historical private detectives". Without their study of all available archive sources, and the sharing of knowledge with fellow enthusiasts, many details of historical military life and practice would have been lost. Much, of course, has

(**Above**) Soldiers of 1.Brandenburg Infantry Regiment No.8 (Life Regiment), a group formed in 1994 from members of the former 2.Brandenburg IR No.12. Today, as in 1813-15, personal equipment varies; during the reorganisation of the Prussian army there were shortages of all kinds of equipment and weapons. Here the re-enactor on the left wears the Prussian Model 1810 knapsack, the man in the middle a "booty" French pack. The officer, right, has a leather officer's model knapsack; note the longer coat tails of officer's uniform.

4

already been lost; but the endless hunt for information is an important part of the fascination of this peculiar hobby.

Even if an interest in military history is foremost, the appeal of the hobby goes much deeper. A trip into history cannot involve military questions only: the warrior or soldier has to be seen in the human context of his times. The re-enactor not only "fights" in his period, he also has to live in it, for days at a time. Dedicated groups devote as much care and attention to their "camp life" as to their drill. They live in reconstructed tents or shelters, cook typical meals with authentic implements, and try to assemble historically accurate tools and equipment. In this way it can sometimes seem possible - if only for a brief moment - to travel back in time for hundreds of years. To the demanding re-enactor the illusion is rare and fleeting; but when it happens, it makes all the effort worth while.

The groups featured here are mostly dedicated to the reconstruction of the period 1813-1815, the years when the German states exploded into patriotic uprisings against the French rule imposed in earlier years by the victorious Napoleon. The authors must admit - cheerfully - to a slight but deliberate ambiguity in the title of this English edition: the contents include not only re-created German Napoleonic troops, but also Napoleonic period troops of other nations, re-created in Germany or encountered by the authors during multinational events. This is partly in order to include, for the sake of balance, such arms of service as cavalry and artillery which are not yet found among the relatively new German groups; and partly to emphasise the diversity of our gatherings.

In the text and captions which follow, general statements

(Above) During large re-enactment events, as here at Leipzig in 1993, tent-cities of considerable size are set up. The "living history" aspect of bivouac life, reconstructed as authentically as possible, offers opportunities for women to participate in the hobby; most German groups disapprove of women dressing as men to serve in the battle-line.

refer to the Prussian army if not otherwise specified. As always when discussing periods before the mid- to late 19th century, it should be borne in mind that quoted regulations represent an "ideal". This was particularly the case with the Prussian forces following the devastating defeats of 1806, when it took decades to achieve uniformity in armament and equipment. It was also true that even in this difficult period many traditional regimental distinctions were preserved. This diversity makes it difficult, in the space available here, to offer more than a representative cross-section; but it also adds to the interest of researching or collecting German militaria.

In Germany today the media and some sections of the public tend to regard any interest in military matters, whether displayed by historians, collectors, or re-enactors, with a degree of suspicion. It is our hope that this book will play a part in the recognition of our hobby as a serious contribution to the study of our past. We are encouraged by recent early steps in constructive co-operation between German living history groups and museums; already common in other countries, this tendency shows that we are moving in the right direction.

Torsten Verhülsdonk
& Carl Schulze 5

The Rebuilding of an Army

The defeats at Jena and Auerstedt in 1806, combined with the French-dictated terms of the subsequent Peace of Tilsit in July 1807, meant the end of the old Prussian army. Of the previous line of 60 infantry regiments and eight fusilier brigades each with three independent battalions, only Regiments Nr.2, 8, 11, 14, 16, 42, 52 and 58 survived the débâcle. On 1 December 1806 King Friedrich Wilhelm III wrote a memorandum concerning the various grievances and shortcomings then obtaining within the army; and in order to build new forces out of the remains of the old army a military reorganisation commission was established on 25 July 1807 under the leadership of Major-General von Scharnhorst. The following year this commission was transformed into the War Ministry.

Between 1807 and 1815 some of the best-known figures in German military history served in the ministry, for example Carl von Clausewitz, August Neidhardt von Gneisenau and Herman von Boyen. One of the major aims of their reforms was to abolish the aristocratic privileges of the officer corps, which was now opened up to any who demonstrated a proper professional knowledge, or exeptional bravery and leadership in the field. In 1810 the first of three Prussian war colleges opened its doors, to train students for the officers' examinations.

The structure of the army was also changed. Prussia was regionally divided into six cantons, and the army into six corresponding brigades. Each brigade was to consist of two infantry and three cavalry regiments plus additional technical troops. The brigade was named after its province - East Prussia, West Prussia, Pommerania, Brandenburg, Lower Silesia and Upper Silesia. The regiments were numbered sequentially, and bore an additional provincial designation. The historic practice of naming regiments after their commanding officer was discontinued. The uniforms were also changed to simpler and more practical designs. Training was restructured; obligatory manuals were issued for all branches of service and for the operations of combined arms. Linear tactics were no longer the only possibility, but were now seen as only one aspect of a "demand-orientated" mix of linear, column and skirmishing tactics.

Following the Peace of Tilsit and the Convention of Paris the withdrawal of French occupation troops was made dependent on a limitation of Prussian army manpower to a total of 42,000 - ten regiments of infantry with 22,000 men, ten regiments or 32 squadrons of cavalry totalling 8,000, a 6,000-man corps of artillery, sappers and miners, plus 6,000 Guard troops.

To create a sufficient reserve of trained soldiers the *Krümper* system was instituted on 6 August 1808. This important reform - from which some historians directly trace the birth of the modern German military system - involved a regular rotation of manpower. After a satisfactory level of training was achieved, intakes of fully trained soldiers were returned to civilian life but with a continuing reserve obligation, while the same number of newly drafted conscripts were given basic training. By this means the Prussian army never had more than 42,000 soldiers under arms at any one time, but could draw upon a substantially larger pool of trained men when the opportunity arose.

(Above left) Prussians of various units, their colours rolled and cased for the march, form a "clump" for all-round defence against cavalry attacks.

(Above) During the 180th anniversary of the Battle of the Nations at Leipzig in 1993, Polish lancers break into the lines of the Colberg Infantry Regiment No.9. As close combat demonstrations always bear some risks, they are only performed following a specific "script" agreed by the groups involved.

(Right) The recreated 1.Brandenburg Infantry Regiment No.8 leave a bivouac in a farm near Waterloo. The men wear their greatcoats or blankets rolled and tied, passing over the right shoulder and knapsack, as typically seen in the field during our period. The bayonet was normally carried fixed; and note red rag plugs in the muzzles, to protect the bore from dirt and rain.
(Photo: Peter J. Nachtigall)

Infantry of the Line

The majority of any armed force has always been provided by the infantry. As in most armies, the Prussian infantry was divided into Guard and Line units, the former normally comprising the oldest and most traditional units, with the smartest drill, the most elaborate uniforms and special insignia. The Guards fulfilled ceremonial duties and were the household troops of the sovereign. Their operational tactics were the same as for the rest of the infantry, but serving with the Guards carried privileges for both rank-and-file and officers.

The infantry was organized in both heavy and light units; the major differences lay not in weapons and equipment, but in training and tactics, which dictated their place in the line of battle. The majority of the infantry units were of the heavy type, which moved and fought in line or battalion column, forming a solid body of troops. On the field of battle they provided the main force and the reserve; and almost invariably it was their behaviour which decided the outcome of the engagement. To move, fight and fire as a cohesive body they needed to be thoroughly trained and drilled.

The élite of the heavy infantry were the "grenadiers", tracing their name back to the days of the first, dangerous handgrenades in the 17th century, when only the best and strongest men were trusted with throwing them. In pitched battle on the open field the handgrenade was virtually forgotten by 1800; but the Grenadiers, armed with regular muskets, formed the flank company of the battalion - and

Grenadier companies were often grouped into élite battalions or regiments. The centre or battalion companies were called "Musketeers". The light troops were named Fusiliers; although armed with the same smoothbore flintlock muskets as the Grenadiers and Musketeers, they were trained as skirmishers. Their task, classically, was to distract and weaken the main mass of the enemy; to fight in open order in wooded or rough terrain; to hit the enemy at his softest point, and to cover the flanks of their own unit.

In Prussia, although the troops in the third rank were trained in skirmishing tactics, very few of them initially received rifles to improve their marksmanship. If ordered to "spread out" *(Schwärmen)* they moved out of the line, and assembled in skirmishing lines in front of their units. About half of them closed with the enemy, forming groups of two called "files"; the two soldiers of a file supported each other, one loading while the other fired. The forming of whole Fusilier regiments, or the concentration of Fusilier companies as a third battalion of each infantry regiment, was to follow at a later date.

Also among the light troops were to be found the Rifles and Jäger ("hunter") battalions, which are discussed in a later chapter.

The distinction between light or heavy infantry was common to all national armies; their tactics and armament were very similar, though their organisation varied. The British army gave their skirmishing troops special insignia and grouped them as a light company on the flank of the infantry battalion; they also designated some complete battalions as light and Rifle troops. French battalions had so-called *Voltigeur* companies, and in addition a number of light infantry regiments (in France, in contrast to Prussia, the "fusilier" was the heavy infantryman).

Uniforms

The practical aspects of the 1807 reorganisation included a new uniform very different from the old Prussian fashion. An order dated 12 November 1807 specified a jacket of dark ("Prussian") blue, double-breasted with two rows of eight yellow metal buttons (the Prussian-German military called all kinds of brass or gilt insignia "yellow", and silver-coloured metal was referred to as "white".) The coat was waist length, tailored tight to accentuate the figure, sometimes with padding in the breast. The sleeves were also very tight and reached further into the shoulder than today, where they were set in pleats. The design of the very tight cuff was called "Brandenburg", featuring a small vertical flap on the outside, closed with three buttons (although the lowest was normally worn open). At the back were two short, wool-lined tails with interior pockets and red "turnbacks" or visible facings; in the small of the rear waist were two buttons. The collar, originally cut open and very high, was suppose to reach the men's ears. Depending upon regiment it was worn stiffened or soft. Initially the coat had only a left shoulderstrap, but on 30 August 1809, with the decision to carry the knapsack by straps over both shoulders rather than slung diagonally, a right shoulderstrap was ordered added. On 26 May 1814 the collar was ordered to be altered, being henceforth shorter and closed in front with three hooks and eyes.

The AKO (Allerhöchste Kabinetts Order - Highest Cabinet Order) dated 5 September 1807 ordered a shako termed the Russian model as headdress, which had been used on an experimental basis before 1806. The felt shako had a leather headband, visor and chinstrap; enlisted men displayed a band of white woollen lace around the top edge, and NCOs a gold band. All branches wore a shako pompon (called a "rose") in white and black wool, the Prussian colours. Musketeers wore the royal cypher in brass; Fusiliers wore a white and black leather cockade, fixed with a button and a strip of wollen lace for enlisted men or brass for NCOs; Grenadiers wore brass eagles of various designs. On 23 December 1808 a black oilcloth shako cover was ordered to be worn for everyday duty and in the field; this often had a fold-down rainflap to protect the neck, and was fixed by cords at the back. Often shakos lacking any of the official decorations were worn permanently covered, but it was not uncommon to display some or all decorations on the cover itself.

For the Russian expedition of 1812, in which Prussian troops were obliged to participate with the Grande Armée, a new shako model was introduced; this had a leather top and two diagonal leather reinforcing strips on each side. This model was already in use with the cavalry, and

proved satisfactory. The style of the pompon was also changed to a more oval shape. The chinstrap was now sometimes replaced by chinscales, officially ordered for all units only in the 1830s.

The reorganisation brought cuts in the amount of baggage allowed to be carried with the army, leading to the abolition of tents. Instead the troops received (under an AKO dated 6 November 1807) a greatcoat, originally abandoned by order of King Friedrich Wilhelm I. This was a grey, calf-length, unlined coat made with five or six pleats in the back, running from the collar downwards, which were tightened by a sewn-in belt. The greatcoat gave protection against rain and cold on the march, and also provided some cover when bivouacking in the open.

The trousers were of grey wool, tight at the calf and closed with three buttons. They were worn with calf-length black cloth gaiters, also closed by a row of cloth-covered buttons. In 1813 a looser fitting design of overalls was issued, the front flap now widened out to the side seams; these were worn over the knee-length black boots which were now sometimes available. In the summer months white linen trousers were worn with short black gaiters. The shoes were of a laced pattern, with hobnails, boots becoming generally available only later.

(Above left) Yellow braid around cuffs and collar distinguishes this member of the Life Regiment as an Unteroffizier or corporal. It was applied around the bottom of the open style of collar, moving to the top edge of the 1814 closed collar. He wears an early pattern knapsack with narrow straps at the shoulders and a loose breast strap. The canteen is of civilian manufacture; it was not until 1867 that a regulation piece became available. The horse belongs to a field grade officer, the only members of infantry units to be mounted.

(Above) Engineer officer in full marching order wearing the 1814 uniform with black velvet closed collar and cuffs bearing silver lace bars. Here he has been given command of infantry for the protection of his technical troops. He wears the officer's knapsack, introduced in 1809 for infantry and 1810 for engineer officers.

(Above right) Infantryman of 2. Pommeranian IR No.9 - beards were not usual in line units. He wears a field cap with a band in corresponding colour to his collar. Canteen and cup are privately purchased. He wears white linen trousers over shoes with short black gaiters.

(Right) The Prussian troops which marched into Russia with Napoleon in 1812 were ordered to wear the Prussian black and white cockade as a recognition sign on the shako cover. Officially this was to be made of painted leather and sewn to the cover, but often the white border was simply painted on the oilcloth. The Russian campaign ended for the Prussians in December 1812 with the Tauroggen convention by which Lt.Gen. Yorck concluded a treaty of neutrality with the Russian Maj.Gen. Diebitsch. (Photo: Peter J. Nachtigall)

11

(Left) Reconstruction of typical hobnailed shoes of the period. They were made "straight-lasted", i.e. there was no difference between the left and right feet, and were changed regularly from foot to foot to ensure equal wear.

(Right) The 1995 Waterloo re-enactment was memorable for its authentic weather conditions: the days before the event were very showery, and on the actual day the weather cleared at 09.30 after a rainy night. In 1815 the artillery and transport had to struggle against the poor condition of the roads, and the advance of the infantry was also delayed. Contemporary sources state that the mud was up to knee deep. Prussian soldiers wearing boots were lucky - most had only low shoes.

(Right) A Colberg infantryman resting during the march; his covered shako is fixed to his knapsack. The plate on the ammunition pouch of Grenadiers and Musketeers showed an eagle over various trophies (see also page 9); Fusiliers did not display a plate.

14

(Above far left) The normal Prussian formation for musketry was a two-rank line, giving concentrated volleys with an increased possibility of hits. The sidearm carried here is the "Old Prussian" Model 1715; note also the absence of bayonet scabbards.

(Above left) Recreated Life Regiment soldier cocking his British-supplied "Brown Bess" musket; a brass Prussian fireshield has been retrospectively fitted around the priming pan to protect his right-hand man from burns. White shoulderstraps distinguish the 1. from the 2. Brandenburg Regiment, who wore red straps.

(Above) French troops advancing in line draw fire from Prussian skirmishers. Recruited from among the best shots, these formed the third rank when not detached to fight in open order.

(Far left & left) The Imperial Russo-German Legion was raised in 1812 in Russia from German-speaking volunteers, mostly Prussian or Rhine Confederation prisoners or stragglers, to assist the Russians against Napoleon and later to carry the fight into Germany; the expense was met by Britain. (The best-known Prussian officer in the Legion was Carl von Clausewitz.) In 1813-14 they served, 8,500 strong, in Corps Wallmoden of the Northern Army; but long pay arrears and uncertainty over their future led to unrest. Eventually all non-Prussian soldiers were offered their discharge, the rest being transferred into Saxon and Berg units as part of the Prussian army. The name was changed to German Legion; in 1815 the remaining infantry regiments were numbered 30 and 31 in the Prussian line, the hussars formed the 8th Lancers, and the Legion was disbanded on 15 April 1815. The Legion's equipment was partly from British stocks. They wore green coats with red turnbacks; battalions were distinguished by the colours of collar and shoulderstraps. The cockade on the Russian shako was red and white.

Landwehr (Militia)

"To my people" - with these words King Friedrich Wilhelm III began his appeal of 17 March 1813, proclaiming the "decree for the organisaton of the militia" and calling his people to arms to overthrow French rule. Under this decree all able-bodied men between 17 and 40 years old and not already serving in the army or one of the volunteer formations were obliged to serve in the militia. The order, based on a draft by Maj.Gen.Gerhard von Scharnhorst, was in practice the beginning of conscription in Prussia, even if at first limited to the duration of that war. Although loosely similar systems existed from 1808 in Austria and 1812 in Russia, the Prussian system differed from those of France and most of her allies in that there were no exemptions for special ranks or groups; no substitution was possible, and the individual could not buy himself out of his obligation.

The raising of the militias followed the provincial organisation, quotas being set by the government in accordance with the population of the province, but the raising of units being delegated to the provincial governments. The Landwehr generally received completely untrained personnel consisting mainly of unmarried volunteers. Only if not enough volunteered to fill the quota were conscripts drawn by lot. The typical age of the militiamen was therefore lower than in later wars. The raising of the units was not always accomplished without problems; but in those provinces scarred by the battles of previous campaigns, such as East Prussia, Kurmark and Neumark, volunteers responded in large numbers to avenge years of oppression.

One interesting feature of militia units was that enlisted men elected their NCOs. The officers, up to company level, were appointed by the local authorities, subject to confirmation by the king; senior officers could still be suggested by the local governments.

The ceasefire, demanded by Austria, which was signed at Pläswitz on 4 June 1813 and which lasted until 10 October that year, was used as an opportunity to train the militia; and many Landwehr units would later distinguish themselves in battle side by side with the regular forces. By the end of the ceasefire 149 battalions were combat-ready. Three to four battalions formed each Landwehr-Infanterie-Regiment, which bore sequential provincial numbers. The battles at Grossbeeren, Katzbach, Hagelberg and Dennewitz in August and September 1813 were their baptism of fire. Between 1813 and 1817 a total of five East Prussian, three West Prussian, three Pommeranian, seven Kurmärkische, three Neumärkische, 15 Silesian, ten

(Above & right) Officer and men of the Landwehr Battalion Höxter - 1st Bn., 5th Westphalian Landwehr Infantry Regiment. Note the green distinctive colour of Westphalia; the white gloves typically worn by officers even in these volunteer battalions, who normally provided their own varied equipment and weapons; and the Landwehr cross cap insignia, its arms bearing the inscription "With God for King and Country".

Westphalian, one Berg'sches, four Elbe, two Upper Saxon, two Thuringian, eight Rhine, five Posensche and one Stralsunder Militia Infantry Regiments were raised.

Uniforms

The dress of the Landwehr was quite simple, consisting of a dark blue *litewka* coat with a double row of buttons, and a collar in the colour of the province - sometimes the cuffs were also faced, or piped, in the provincial colour. Military coats not being available in sufficient numbers, civilian "Sunday" coats in blue or black, with an added collar in provincial colour, were acceptable. When even these proved hard to find, all cuts and colours of civilian coats might be seen in the ranks. At first the shoulderstraps were in battalion colours - white, red, yellow and blue for the 1st to 4th respectively. A regimental number might be sewn to or embroidered on the straps, but these was not worn by all units. Landwehr regiments raised later in the war - e.g. the 5th Westphalian, formed in 1814 - wore shoulderstraps in regimental colours like those of the Line infantry.

Grey trousers or overalls were not available for most units, so white linen and civilian trousers were worn. Shoes, boots and gaiters were used as available, but

most footwear too represented what the individual happened to own at the time of his enlistment. The prescribed headdress was a visored cap with a blue crown and a band in provincial colour; on this band was worn a leather cockade, its outer edge painted white; above this a white metal cross was sewn to the crown, bearing the wording "With God for King and Country 1813". Sometimes these crosses were simply cut out of tin or even cloth. The shape of the cap roughly followed that of the shako, having a stiffened crown slightly larger in diameter at the top; when unstiffened the crown collapsed into a shape which has since become familiar among armies the world over. The coloured piping around the crown was instituted by an order of 31 May 1814.

Equipping the Landwehr presented serious problems; provincial governments were short of every kind of necessity. Without flintlock muskets in sufficient numbers, in some battalions pikes were issued to the men in the front rank, and contemporary sources also show troops armed with agricultural tools. Muskets slowly became available for all battalions, but not uniformly from army arsenals: all kinds of firearms were pressed into use - war booty, foreign aid, or even weapons built from scrap and various replacement parts. The situation with sidearms was no better; in 1813 there were not enough sabres to equip all NCOs with this distinction of their rank, so all kinds were used ranging from old Prussian 1715 models to war booty. Militiamen were even ordered to carry axes and spades as sidearms.

The leather equipment was as for the regular infantry, either black or white in colour. For carrying their personal belongings a haversack was often the only thing available, as very few regular army cowhide knapsacks reached the Landwehr. Through a British aid programme some tarred canvas Trotter knapsacks were supplied, but the soft French knapsacks were much more sought-after than the uncomfortable wooden-framed Trotter.

(Below) Knapsack and haversack contents of a Wehrmann (militiaman), with personal belongings naturally similar to those of Line soldiers. A spare pair of shoes was real luxury, and clogs were often the only footwear available. At bottom left lies the weapon cleaning kit consisting of an oil bottle, a tin of powdered brick, and perhaps a spring clamp. On his spare shirt lie sewing and writing materials, a newspaper and a pack of cards. Beside the cup, plate and cutlery are a pair of drawers and knitted socks placed on the laundry bag. Below these at right, on a linen towel, is his washing kit including a toothbrush and toothpowder; left of this in the small leather bag is a tin of dubbin for the leather equipment. The brushes are for cleaning clothes and equipment. At bottom right are clothes pegs and a line, and a bag with flint, steel and tinder.

(Right) The *litewka* coat was cut similarly to contemporary civilian coats, tailored snugly to the waist. The sleeves reached further into the shoulders than today, with many pleats.

(Below) The equipment of the Landwehr militiaman, laid out on his blanket. His personal belongings are packed into the haversack and knapsack; note the field cap and service cap at top right. The weapon is a captured French Model 1777 with a Prussian-added pan shield. The sabre is an "Old Prussian" model, carried in a double frog with (unusually for the Landwehr) a bayonet scabbard. In the ammunition pouch are paper cartridges, some spare flints, oil and a combination tool. The hatchet and flute are typical personal additions.

(Above) The Landwehr battalions were formed, sketchily equipped and trained over a period of a few months, from volunteers without military experience; yet they sometimes fought impressively well. One obvious difficulty was the shortage of standardised weapons, and consequent problems of ammunition supply; Prussian, British, French and other muskets of differing calibres would be carried within a battalion or even a single company. Dating from 1814, the Battalion Höxter was one of the last units raised to fight Napoleon.

(Right) It seems to have been common for militiamen to be bearded. He is armed with a Brown Bess, delivered by Britain in large quantities. It was ordered that the Landwehr receive black leather equipment, as worn by Jägers and Fusiliers, but given the widespread shortages of all types of necessities it was common for white crossbelts to be issued instead.

(Above) These photos of a member of the 5th Westphalians illustrate perfectly the appearance of a well-equipped Landwehr volunteer in 1815. He wears the *litewka* with collar and cuffs in the green indicating Westphalia, and green shoulderstraps, this time denoting the 5th Regiment. His cap is of typical Landwehr shape; shakos were not available (in fact there was an order to collect any discarded French shakos for issue to militia units). Grey woollen trousers were a rarity, white linen being commonly used, with laced shoes and short gaiters. His equipment

consists of a black cartridge pouch and an infantry sabre carried on white crossbelts. The knapsack is the French cowhide type. Strapped to it might be a blanket or, if available, a greatcoat; and note the hatchet.

(Right) Note the design of the sleeve, narrow at the forearm but wide and puffed at the shoulder. The cap has the crown piping in provincial band colour, introduced in 1814. The national cockade was made from leather and sewn to the cap, as was the metal Landwehr cross. The musket is a modified French M1777.

(Above) To defend themselves against attacking cavalry smaller groups could only form a "clump", back to back and facing in all directions.

(Left) The black and white lace indicates the rank of Unteroffizier (corporal). Just visible under the coat is the waistcoat which was common in this period.

(Above) These Silesian militiamen, with their varied uniforms and muskets, pikes and even agricultural tools, provide a good example of the Landwehr's appearance in 1813. Yellow was the distinctive colour of Silesia, the red shoulderstraps denoting the 2nd Battalion of the regiment. Note the locks of two muskets wrapped with a piece of oily rag as protection from damp. (Photo: Peter J. Nachtigall)

(Left) The shortage of knapsacks meant that simple linen bags were often issued to the militia.

(Left) This Silesian militia officer wears a coat of similar cut to that of Line officers but without cuff flaps; the distinctive colours were the same as for enlisted men. The epaulette came into use as the mark of commissioned rank in 1813; since 1808 officers had worn shoulderstraps as for enlisted men but with braid in different styles to denote exact rank. He is armed with the Fusilier's sabre in the brass scabbard which was forbidden shortly after the Wars of Liberation. His cap is a non-regulation private item: normally band and piping would also be yellow.

(Right) The Kurmark Landwehr regiments had "crab-red" distinctions and yellow buttons; the blue shoulder straps of this NCO denote the 4th Battalion of his regiment. His leather equipment is regulation black; and just visible, hanging from the "Old Prussian" infantry sabre, is the black and white NCOs' swordknot.

(Left) Unteroffizier of the 4th Battalion, 3rd Kurmark Landwehr Infantry Regiment offering a helping hand to a "wounded" comrade.

(Left) The re-enactment hobby involves much more than simply recreating battles. An illusion of time travel also demands a really careful "living history" display, authentically recreating day to day routine; and a historical bivouac, like this Westphalian militia camp, is essential.

(Above) Westphalian, Kurmark and Silesian Landwehr forming a square at Waterloo. This formation was very effective against cavalry if the soldiers kept their nerve and held their fire until the riders were at short range; if they fired too early the effect was minimal, and the cavalry could reach them before they reloaded. The regimental colours in the background do not belong to a militia unit, being of the black and white design typical of Line infantry. (Photo: Peter J. Nachtigall)

(**Left**) On their 1995 journey to Waterloo the "Prussian Brigade" were followed by baggage wagons with canteen women and camp-followers, who cared for the soldiers' wellbeing during this historic march.
(**Above**) The 5th Westphalian Landwehr on the march to Waterloo. For the 180th anniversary in 1995 several groups of the Napoleonische Gesellschaft, together with British cavalry, followed the historical route of the Prussian army via Ligny and Wavre over several days before the main battle re-enactment.

Jägers, Rifles & Volunteer Units

A lthough few re-enactors have yet recreated Jäger units, these élite troops deserve mention.

The formation of regular Jäger units dated back to 1744 and the Feldjäger Corps raised by Friedrich II. In the campaigns of earlier times units of professional hunters and foresters were raised for temporary service, but in peacetime these field-crafty marksmen were sent back to their hunting-grounds. The Jägers always proved reliable if employed according to their special abilities, rather than being forced into the rigid tactical matrix of the Line troops; but incompetent officers and unimaginative tactics often took a bloody toll.

With the personal protection of Friedrich the Great, who understood the strengths and limitations of his Jägers, their fortunes improved as their special employment was consolidated into the army's tactical doctrine. Important improvements were introduced by attached Hessian officers, experienced in the use of light troops from their British service in the American War of Independence. The Jägers' training became more related to the contemporary realities of battle - especially after a master of the "small war", Major von Yorck, took command of the Jäger-Regiment in 1799.

In the 1806 battles of Jena and Auerstedt the Jägers were not involved, but distinguished themselves during the fighting withdrawals which followed. Blücher's capitulation at Lübeck and the capture of the wounded Colonel von Yorck meant the end of the Jäger-Regiment. In November 1808 an AKO from Friedrich Wilhelm III resurrected them; a 1st or Guard Jäger Battalion was established in Brandenburg, a 2nd or East Prussian Jäger Battalion plus a Rifles (Schützen) Battalion in Silesia. In 1814 a Guard Rifles Battalion was recruited in Neufchatel, a former Swiss territory; there followed a Jäger battalion raised in Magdeburg in June 1815, and a Rhine Rifles Battalion that October.

Uniforms and armament

The Jäger uniform during the Wars of Liberation was cut as for the Line infantry. The coat was dark green with yellow buttons; the collar, Swedish cuffs, turnbacks and piping were red. The Guard battalion wore yellow lace bars on collar and cuffs. The Silesian Rifles wore black collars and shoulderstraps with red piping, their cuffs being of Brandenburg form, black with red piping and a green flap with the usual three buttons. The Guard Rifles wore black collars piped red with yellow lace bars, red shoulderstraps and French cuffs - similar to the Brandenburg type but having a curved flap. The units raised in 1815 had shoulderstraps in yellow (Magdeburg) and red (Rhine); and the Silesian Rifles changed their black straps to white.

Volunteer Jäger attached to 1. Brandenburg Infantry Regiment No.8. The uniform of the Volunteer Jäger was similar to that of the regular Jäger, though personally provided, and therefore varying in quality and completeness according to the wealth of the individual. The colours and style of collar, cuffs and shoulderstraps followed those of the parent regiment. Note the narrow cut of the sleeve and the unfastened flap button. This rifle - typically for a volunteer - is a civilian hunting weapon, and has no attachment for the sword-bayonet.

All battalions wore the infantry shako, but without lace. The Guards emblem was a brass star; the East Prussians had a cockade retained by a V of lace, the Silesians by a strip of yellow-coloured tin. For parade the shako was dressed with green cord and a black feather plume. The 1812 model shako with leather top was as for Line infantry; now all battalions except Guards wore the cockade behind a strip of yellow tin. Trousers were of infantry pattern; the Jägers wore them tucked inside knee-length boots, but the Rifles wore shoes with gaiters.

The armament of these light battalions differed from their Line counterparts: a shorter flintlock with a rifled barrel and rudimentary sights for two or three different ranges, giving much more accuracy than the smoothbore Line musket. Due to the tight fit of the ball in the rifled barrel loading was complicated and time-consuming. A weapon accurate to two or three times the normal range; the long-practised skills (in theory, at least) of the tracker and hunter in wooded or broken terrain - all these made the Jäger the perfect soldier for outposts or rearguards, for sniping or reconnaissance.

The leather equipment of Jägers and Rifles was black

and worn in a fashion similar to Line infantry. The sidearm was not a sabre but a "hunting sword", a type of large, straight sword-bayonet; while this could be fixed to the rifle it was done only in a real emergency, as the heavy sword could bend the barrel in close combat.

The cartridge pouch was smaller than for Line infantry, as the number of paper cartridges carried, for use with the so-called "rolling ball", was low - they were only used against a sudden enemy threat, e.g. from cavalry. In this pouch they carried about 60 loose bullets, which were loaded carefully wrapped in a patch taken from a patch-box in the buttstock. A brass powder flask was carried in a soft leather pocket on the front of the crossbelt, secured by a chain, as were the picker and brush for cleaning the pan and touchhole of the rifle. They also carried - in the haversack, or slung on a cord - a small wooden mallet to drive the patched ball into the muzzle. To secure the pouch and sword crossbelts from flapping as they moved the Jägers wore a black waistbelt over them. The Rifles battalions used, like the infantry, cowhide knapsacks; but the Jägers had a special knapsack covered in badger fur, with a badger head reconstructed on the flap.

With the defeat of the *Grande Armée* in the Russian winter of 1812, Prussia saw a chance to overthrow French domination. Before the Landwehr was constituted, on 3 February 1813, a decree was published calling for the raising of volunteer Jäger detachments. Every infantry battalion and cavalry regiment was to form a company of about 200 volunteers. The training of these men - mostly from the middle classes - was done by selected personnel, as the Volunteer Jägers were designated as replacements for NCOs and officers in regular units. By getting volunteers from the educated classes into the forces, the authorities intended to broaden the general acceptance of the military among the population as a whole. The high casualties suffered in the subsequent campaigns meant that by the end of the Wars of Liberation a large number of regular regimental officers were indeed promoted Volunteer Jägers.

The honour of serving in a Volunteer Jäger detachment cost not only patriotic dedication but also a heavy purse, as the individual had to provide his own uniform, weapon and equipment - and in Volunteer Mounted Jäger units, his horse as well. Enthusiasm was great but financal resources limited, so money and equipment were collected all over the country to equip the volunteer companies.

Volunteer Jägers were supposed to wear regular Jäger uniforms but with collar, cuffs and shoulderstraps in the colours of the battalion (e.g. dark red collar and cuffs, white shoulderstraps, for the Volunteer Jäger Company of the 6th Infantry Regiment [1st West Prussian]). Since they brought their own weapons, a wide range of military and civilian rifles and hunting swords were seen in the ranks; and muskets were also used when rifles were not available.

*　　　　*　　　　*

With the growing number of foreigners appearing to join the fight against Napoleon, the formation of irregular "free corps" was ordered; the best-known of these was Lützow's Free Corps. Although all personnel of this unit were termed Jägers, this was a purely honorific title - very few Free Corps had real Volunteer Jäger detachments, armed with rifles and marked as potential officers in regular units.

(Left) The Guards Jäger Battalion [illegible] yellow lace bars on cuffs and collar. To secure the crossbelt equipment an additional black waistbelt was worn. The powder flask is carried in a thin leather pocket on the front of the pouch belt, secured by a chain, as was the picker and brush. The scabbard of the hunting-sword was of natural brown colour. This NCO re-enactor wears the field cap intead of the heavy shako.

(Below) Saxon light infantry at Leipzig, 1993. These troops were armed with muskets made at the Suhl factory, and some rifles might also have been carried, since the remnants of the Jäger battalion were used to form the light infantry. This shako cover of calfhide was a Saxon peculiarity; some contemporary drawings show it worn with the complete shako furniture attached.

(Above) Lock of a civilian rifle of the period, typical of the weapons used by the volunteer companies. Note the entirely characteristic fouling of burnt powder around the flintlock action. This weapon has the "set-" or "hair-trigger" common on quality weapons in our period. The front trigger was squeezed first, taking up nearly all the pressure; after fixing on a target the rifleman needed to apply only very light pressure on the second trigger to fire the action.

(Left) An NCO (Oberjäger) of the Volunteer Jäger Battalion "von Reiche", which was distinguished by green coats with red collars and cuffs and light green shoulderstraps. The shako, of standard 1812 pattern with leather top and diagonal side reinforcement strips, is furnished with chinscales and a green cord; some sources state that the unit also wore a falling horsehair plume. The Berlin contingent of this Free Corps wore green trousers with a broad red stripe instead of the normal grey ones. The hunting-sword crossbelt bore an oval plate inscribed "Berliner Freiwillige".

The King's German Legion

N ot all German states submitted to Napoleon without resistance; and one example of a continuous struggle against the aggressor was provided by the Electorate of Hanover (raised to the dignity of a Kingdom in 1814). Although the Hanoverian army was disbanded after the Elbe conventions the will to resist the conqueror was undiminished. In contrast to e.g. Westphalia, which was obliged to accept one of Bonaparte's relatives as king and put its army under French command, many Hanoverians refused to submit. Hoping to continue the fight for their homeland side by side with the British, they emigrated in some numbers to England - their ruler, the Elector, was also King George III of England.

Under the leadership of the Duke of Cambridge, recruiting of volunteers started in 1803; and the King's German Regiment was raised on 13 October that year, under the initial command of the Scottish Lt.Col.Colin Halkett and the Hanoverian Col.von der Decken. The numbers of volunteers coming via Hamburg and Heligoland were so great, however, that the decision was taken to raise units of all arms of service; and on 19 December the regiment was renamed as the King's German Legion. The call for recruits in the northern parts of Germany, and the will to escape French military service, prompted a continued flow of volunteers from various German states, particularly after Britain and France resumed hostilities (though 75 per cent of the total of some 15,000 volunteers would be Hanoverian).

Within little more than two years the Legion comprised two Light and eight Line battalions of infantry, three light and two heavy cavalry regiments, plus one artillery regiment with two horse and four foot batteries; given the complications of recruitment, however, the strength of these units was sometimes well below that of comparable British units. The uniforms, weapons and equipment of the Legion came entirely from British stocks, but with some traditional Hanoverian peculiarities.

Training was carried out according to the Hanoverian manuals; all orders were given in German, only guard and parade duties being performed to English commands. In 1806 the artillery got a British manual, as they were placed under command of the Board of Ordnance. The 1807 cavalry regulations featured entirely bilingual commands; in the same year the infantry were ordered to adopt the British regulations instead of the Hanoverian, but this was never fully achieved. (The interesting 1813 manual for the Light Battalions is a compendium of Hanoverian and British elements which also draws on practical experience from various campaigns.)

The 1st and 2nd Light Battalions KGL took part in all major British campaigns between 1805 and 1815. The

(**Above**) Although the KGL's enlisted men and officers were mostly from the Elector of Hanover's army which had been disbanded in 1803, the complete equipment was of British origin. The buglehorn, worn on the shako and painted on the side of the knapsack in the 2nd Light Battalion, remains an international symbol for light infantry troops to the present day. The wooden canteen, of the British army's "Italian" pattern, is marked to the Legion, the battalion, the company, and the soldier's individual number.

(**Right**) Rifleman of the 2nd Light Bn., KGL in marching order. On campaign the soldier had to carry equipment, ammunition and rations which could easily total a load of 60 pounds. To allow some freedom of movement to the arms and take the pressure off the shoulder joints the British army's Trotter knapsack had a breaststrap; but when this was fastened it put dangerous pressure on the lungs, making breathing difficult. The folded blanket was sometimes carried beneath the knapsack flap, sometimes between the knapsack and the body for protection against the hard wooden frame.

uniforms of the Light Batallions differed from those of the Line in cut and colour, and even these two units displayed battalion-specific differences. Since as yet the only KGL unit recreated by a German re-enactment group is the 2nd Light Battalion, only their uniform is discussed in detail here (though at the time of writing Line infantry and artillery groups are beginning to form).

Uniform of the 2nd Light Battalion

The unit wore dark green coats (or more exactly, "coatees") cut very similarly to those of the British 95th Rifles, with three rows of pewter buttons on the breast decorated with a buglehorn and the battalion number. These coats, unlike the red uniforms of the Line battalions, did not have tails. Collar, cuffs and shoulderstraps were black. One special distinction of light troops were the padded black shoulder "wings", but these were worn only by the 1st Light Battalion; the 2nd wore large black tufts sewn into the shoulder seam. The grey trousers were of standard British manufacture; white linen was substituted for hot weather.

The shako was of "stovepipe" shape with a leather top, band and visor; to waterproof the felt body (as there were no covers available) it was painted with black oil colour. The badge was a white metal buglehorn; a green woollen plume was fixed behind a black cockade with a battalion button; and a black cord both decorated the shako and secured it against loss, being carried down to fasten to a coat button.

In the 2nd Battalion, in disobedience to regulations, the men were allowed to wear moustaches; the light infantry regarded themselves as having a direct affinity with the light cavalry, who traditionally wore moustaches. This echoing of light horse styles is also very clear in the officers' uniforms: their headdress was the mirleton, their richly braided coat resembled the dolman, they tended to wear riding breeches or overalls with reinforcements, and instead of an infantry officer's sword they favoured the cavalry sabre (and sometimes even a sabretasche).

All leather equipment was black, but only a part of the battalion were armed with Baker rifles, so the equipment differed for these "Sharpshooters". The battalion companies, armed with the Brown Bess musket of India pattern, wore crossbelts supporting the cartridge pouch and socket bayonet. The Sharpshooters, armed with Bakers, had one crossbelt for the pouch but carried the sword-bayonet on a waistbelt, together with a small pouch for loose bullets. The powderhorn was slung on a green cord, running through loops on the crossbelt. Haversack, canteen and knapsack were of British pattern.

The number of Sharpshooters was increased frequently, as the capacity of Baker's factory and the budget of the Crown allowed - compared to a Brown Bess the Baker rifle was extremely expensive. Initially only one man in every six was armed with it; in 1808 about 30 per cent in the Light Battalions carried them; and by the 1815 campaign it seems that every one of "Halkett's Green Germans" was armed with the rifle.

Equipment of a KGL 2nd Light Bn "Sharpshooter", armed with the Baker rifle (which only gradually replaced the musket throughout the battalion). In his ammunition pouch he normally carried 40 made-up paper cartridges for rapid loading in emergencies; some loose balls; spare flints; a combination stripping tool; a "worm" ramrod tip for drawing charges; a swab ramrod tip for attaching cleaning rags; and a powder measure. The powderhorn, for normal loading, was slung on a green cord passing through loops on his crossbelt. Another 20 loose balls were carried in the small pouch on the waistbelt, and loading patches in the compartment in the rifle's buttstock. The canteen and haversack were standard British issue, as was the navy biscuit or "ammunition bread". The sword-bayonet was carried on the waistbelt. His personal belongings include flint and steel with a small tinder box, a salt box, a cup, a bottle-opener and smoking kit.

Knapsack contents of a KGL rifleman. Trotter's patent knapsack was made from lacquered canvas with a wooden frame, giving the pack a smart appearance even if empty but being uncomfortable to carry when fully packed. Greatcoat and D-section mess tin were strapped onto the knapsack, everything else went into it. Note here the field cap, undress jacket, socks, underwear, spare shoes, gloves, eating and washing kit, cleaning brushes, buttonstick, packets of reserve ammunition, and personal belongings - a tankard, playing cards, etc.

(Above) The long Baker sword-bayonet compensated for the relative shortness of the rifle compared to a musket when it came to hand-to-hand combat. Due to its weight, however, and the weak bayonet catch, it was only carried fixed in an emergency.

(Above right) Here the complete shako furniture is clearly visible; the cord was buttoned to the breast to prevent loss of the headgear. The collar was open, and between shirt and jacket collar a neck stock was worn. The large black wool tufts at the ends of the shoulderstraps were peculiar to the 2nd Light Battalion.

(Right) This pioneer of the 2nd Light Bn. wears the extra equipment more or less standard for this appointment in all European armies: leather gloves and apron, and a cased felling axe. He is armed with a short carbine.

(Above) In the beginning only the best shots were armed with the Baker rifle, although the whole battalion seems to have had them by the time of Waterloo. With the Baker hits at more than 300 yards' range were possible - a distance at which only the unluckiest man could be hit by a smoothbore musket ball. British rifle training included a variety of firing positions; this use of the shako as a secure rest might enable our marksman of "Halkett's Green Germans" to pick off an enemy artillery crew or a commanding officer.

(Left) The lock of the Baker rifle, as also used by the British Rifle regiments - the 60th and 95th.

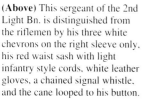

(Above) This sergeant of the 2nd Light Bn. is distinguished from the riflemen by his three white chevrons on the right sleeve only, his red waist sash with light infantry style cords, white leather gloves, a chained signal whistle, and the cane looped to his button.

(Right, top & bottom) Sergeant and private of the 2nd Light Bn. wearing the standard style of British army greatcoat. The former's rank is still visible at some distance, from his chevrons and red sash. Less obvious is another mark of his status, the collar and cuffs in the black facing colour of the two KGL light battalions.

(Far right) The smallest operational group in the light infantry was the skirmishing file of two riflemen. Dispersed over an area of broken or wooded country, or under cover around a bridge or crossroads, a single company of riflemen could hold up much larger enemy conventional forces. Each man supported the other, one loading while the other took aim, so that in theory one rifle was always ready to fire. Here a file pose in an echo of the famous contemporary Hamilton- Smith print. The kneeling marksman has passed his left arm through the rifle sling to brace his aim.

(Above) June 1815-June 1995: for the 180th anniversary of Waterloo members of the recreated 2nd Light Battalion, King's German Legion had the opportunity to "fight" on historic ground. Commanded by their Major Baring, the original 2nd Light Bn. defended the farmhouse of La Haye Sainte, the strategic strongpoint isolated in front of the centre of Wellington's line, against overwhelming odds. When several urgent requests for ammunition resupply brought no result they fought to the last round, the survivors fighting their way back to the Allied lines at the point of the bayonet.

(Left) Officers' uniforms of the 2nd Light Bn. closely resembled those of the British 95th Rifles. With the mirleton, the braided dolman and reinforced overalls, and the sharply curved sabre, he looks more like a hussar than an infantry officer.

Brunswick

Another German contingent fighting alongside the British forces during the Peninsular and Waterloo campaigns with distinction and bravery were the "Black Band" - the troops of Friedrich Wilhelm, Duke of Brunswick-Lüneburg-Oels.

Interestingly, there was no direct link between the dynasties; but with the death of his father as a Prussian field marshal on the field of Auerstedt in 1806 the new duke lost his duchy, which became part of the French-ruled Kingdom of Westphalia. In exile in Austrian Bohemia, the duke began in February 1809 to raise an army. Austria officially supplied him with weapons and equipment to recruit 1,000 infantrymen, 1,000 hussars and an artillery battery with four guns. In 1809 the Brunswickers fought side by side with the Austrians until the ceasefire in July.

The Duke of Brunswick was now in an apparently hopeless situation; but he did not feel bound by the Austro-French peace negotiations. He decided to withdraw his troops along the river Weser, right through Westphalia and northern Germany to the coast, to embark on British warships for England. The response of the people of his former territories was not as he had hoped, but he was able to some extent to replace his losses with volunteers and deserters from Westphalian units. In 1810 the duke's infantry unit, now called the Brunswick-Oels Jägers, was send via Portugal to Spain to fight with Wellington's British army, where they remained until 1814. The cavalry was reorganized and was send to Spain in 1813, taking part in the Sicily landings in 1814. The new situation caused by the Battle of the Nations at Leipzig in October 1813 led to the discharge of the Brunswick infantry from British service in December 1814. The duke regained his duchy in 1813, and immediately started raising a new army.

In January 1814 his first new troops were two companies of "Gelernte Jäger" (professional foresters); the troops returned from England provided two other Light companies, and together these men formed an Avantgarde (vanguard) battalion. A new Leib-Bataillon (life guard battalion) was raised on a cadre of Peninsular veterans. By the Waterloo campaign in 1815 the Brunswick army comprised a Light Infantry Brigade of these two units plus three numbered Light Battalions; a Line Infantry Brigade with three numbered battalions; a five-battalion Reserve Infantry Brigade, and a Landwehr. A hussar regiment and a lancer squadron were newly raised, since the cavalry contingent under British command was not discharged until mid-1815. Also new were one foot and one horse artillery batteries of eight pieces each. Apart from the Reserves all regular units of the "Black Duke's" army were involved in the battles of the Waterloo campaign, the duke himself falling in action at Quatre Bras.

Uniforms

When he raised his troops in 1809 Duke Friedrich Wilhelm followed a rather unusual scheme, dressing them entirely in black uniforms; the shakos and the hussars' sabretasches bore white metal death's-heads, and the Brunswickers' war-cry and the motto on some flags was "Victory or death". The infantry coat was strange, being cut to the length of a *litewka* but braided on the breast like a cavalry dolman. The cavalry wore a true dolman with more elaborate braiding and cuffs. After reorganisation in England the infantry received short, tailless coatees, now even more similar to a dolman, with light blue collars, cuffs and shoulderstraps. With the raising of new troops in 1814 light blue remained the colour of the Leib-Bataillon, other distinctive colours being given to the new battalions.

Their sinister black uniforms earned the Brunswickers the nickname "The Black Band", and their commander that of "The Black Duke". This re-enactor recreates an officer of either the Brunswick-Oels Jägers in British service in the Peninsula, or the later Leib-Bataillon of the 1815 campaign - the uniforms were similar, the braided jacket and trousers black with light blue distinctions. The shako was decorated with a death's-head plate and a falling black horsehair plume with a knot at the top.

(Above) Re-enactors present an impression of the Leib-Bataillon as they might have looked in 1815. The officer's jacket has black embroidery on the collar and forearms and much more elaborate chest braiding than on other ranks' uniform.

(Above right) The Brunswickers' lacquered brown knapsack was painted with a running horse and the motto NUNQUAM RETRORSUM. The British canteens were painted with "BLJ" for Braunschweig-Lauenburg'sche Jäger. They were armed with the Brown Bess musket.

(Right) A Brunswicker adjusting his shako; for rank-and-file this had black leather chinscales. Note that the blue battalion distinction is repeated in the piping down the seams of the trousers.

(Above) Brunswick troops charging side by side with British units during the 1995 Waterloo event.

(Right) The recreation of Napoleonic Wars cavalry units in Germany is only just beginning. The obstacles are far greater than those facing the infantry re-enactor: the cost of keeping and transporting a horse schooled well enough to perform safely in mock battles is very high, and few suitably skilled riders have yet entered the hobby. For good cavalry groups the enthusiast must look to France and England, for the time being at least. This individual Brunswick hussar officer re-enactor, riding with a comrade of the 15th Hussars from England, shows what could be achieved in the way of uniform.

Saxony

The history of the Saxon army is very complex, and can only be touched upon briefly here.

Although the relationship between Prussia and Saxony was somewhat cool due to earlier wars, in 1806 they fought as allies against the French; but 20,000 Saxons could not prevent the defeats of Jena and Auerstedt. In contrast to the flight of the remains of the Prussian army, the Saxon units are described by contemporary sources retreating from the field in perfect order in battalion column with their bands playing, and every French infantry and cavalry attack was beaten off with drill-ground precision.

The Electorate of Saxony was raised to a Kingdom by Napoleon; the new King Friedrich August was forced into a military coalition and obliged to contribute 20,000 men if called upon. In 1807 the first 6,000 Saxon troops were sent to fight for the French at Danzig, Heilsberg and Friedland. Two years later another contingent, 16,000 strong, marched against Austria as IX Corps of the French army. Napoleon preferred using foreigners as cannonfodder, and as the Saxons were renowned as good soldiers they were sent against fiercely defended Austrian positions at Wagram in July. On the first day alone the Saxons suffered 40 per cent casualties.

In 1810 the Saxon army was complete restructured along French lines, with new organisation, tactical training and uniforms. Their next campaign was the invasion of Russia in 1812; in February Saxony mobilized two infantry divisions, which marched into Russia as Napoleon's VII Corps in July. During this campaign the Saxons fought with varied success, usually against overwhelming odds. The retreat of the *Grande Armée* caused a division of Saxony, part being occupied by Russian troops, part still by the French. Shortly before and during the Battle of the Nations at Leipzig in October 1813 complete Saxon battalions and regiments, with their commanders, defected to the Allied forces.

After Napoleon's defeat King Friedrich August of Saxony was imprisoned for collaboration, and lost great parts of his kingdom and his army to Prussia. The Saxon army was again restructered, incorporating the militia and volunteer formations of 1813; further troops from the Russo-German Legion were used to bring the decimated battalions back to strength.

(Above) A grenadier of the Infantry Regiment "Prinz Maximilian" in the 1810 pattern uniform. Following the forced alliance with France the uniforms of the Saxon army copied French models. The white coat was of this typical cut, with the front closed by hooks-and-eyes and cut away at the belly to reveal a waistcoat. Regimental distinctions were by coloured piping, cuffs and lapels; the shoulderstraps were white with coloured piping, sewn into the collar seam with the button placed in the "duck's-foot" shaped outer end. The French shako bore a crowned plate with the sovereign's cypher "FA" for Friedrich August; the Saxon cockade was white, the woollen tuft and cord for Grenadier companies red, and white for all other infantry; all ranks wore metal chinscales.

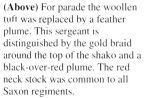

(Above) For parade the woollen tuft was replaced by a feather plume. This sergeant is distinguished by the gold braid around the top of the shako and a black-over-red plume. The red neck stock was common to all Saxon regiments.

(Above right) These Grenadiers carry the infantry sabre of French pattern. Note on the sergeant's forearm the gold braid diagonal stripe, backed with regimental facing colour, which denotes his rank.

(Right) Further details of the shako furniture posed by a Grenadier of the Infantry Regiment "Prinz Maximilian".

(Left) The two Grenadier companies of the Saxon regiment "Prinz Maximilian" were amalgamated to form the Grenadier Battalion "von Spiegel", which was almost completely wiped out in Russia. On sentry duty around their camp in autumn 1812, these Grenadiers show their piped turnbacks decorated in the French fashion with grenade badges in regimental facing colour. The cartridge pouches for Grenadiers bore a brass grenade insignia; Musketeers displayed the sovereign's "FA" cypher on the flap.

(Above & above right) In 1810 Saxony fielded two regiments of light infantry (termed a Corps); this re-enactor depicts a Jäger of the 1st Light Infantry Regiment. The coat was dark green with a black collar and cuffs piped in red; it is worn here with trousers of light ticking material, quite often seen used for fatigue clothing in several Continental armies. The standard infantry shako is covered here - note the rain flap. Leather equipment was black; the pouch flap was decorated with a buglehorn badge, which was also worn by Jägers as the shako insignia instead of the normal plate. His sidearms are a hunting-sword and a bayonet for his Suhl musket; the knapsack is of French origin.

(Right) Only the Grenadier Leibgarde Regiment wore red coats, with yellow facings and white buttons. Instead of shoulder straps the regiment wore small white fringed epaulettes. The shako was decorated with a white cord and a horsehair plume; for parade a fur cap was substituted.

47

(Above) Recreation of Grenadiers of the Infantry Regiment "Steindel", distinguished by green facings. (This was also the facing colour of the Infantry Regiment "Prinz Friedrich August"; so "Steindel" wore white metal buttons, and "Prinz Friedrich August" yellow.) The sidearm is the Saxon infantry sabre for Grenadiers; the man in the middle with apron and belt is a Pioneer. All wear parade plumes.

(Right) Impression of Saxon Grenadiers engaged in a night combat in Russia, wearing grey greatcoats. One man has a Musketeer pouch with crowned cypher plate.

Austria

Austria was, after Prussia, the second "German" power on the Continent, and a serious obstacle to Napoleon's politics of expansion. The Hapsburg rulers of this multi-racial state confronted French armies often, though with variable success.

The first severe defeats for the Austrians at Napoleon's hands were the battles of Marengo and Hohenlinden in 1800, and the subsequent peace cost the Holy Roman Empire territories on the left bank of the Rhine ceded to France. War broke out again in 1805; the capitulation of a large Austrian army at Ulm and the capture of Vienna was followed on 2 December by the "Battle of the Three Emperors" at Austerlitz, Napoleon's devastating victory over Alexander I of Russia and Franz II of Austria. The Peace of Pressburg cost Austria further territories, and in August 1806 the Emperor Franz was forced to lay down the crown of the Holy Roman Empire.

Half-hearted attempts at administrative and military reform in 1798/99 and 1805 were now pursued more vigorously. In 1809, under the leadership of the Archduke Karl, the next passage of arms at Aspern and Essling was decided for Austria; but failure to exploit this victory proved fatal, and only six weeks later the Austrians were forced to capitulate at Wagram after some days of fierce fighting. The Peace of Schönbrunn brought France yet more Austrian territory; and to secure his position in this part of Europe, Napoleon married the Archduchess Marie Louise.

For the Russian expedition of 1812 Austria fielded an auxiliary corps of 30,000 men. In August 1813 she declared war on France, and fought at Leipzig in October. During the Hundred Days no Austrian troops reached the Low Countries in time for the final struggle.

Uniforms

At large scale re-enactment events one normally finds two kinds of "Austrian" troops, so only these will be mentioned here. One large group recreates the so-called "German" infantry of the Austrian army, fielding Grenadiers and Fusiliers of various regiments; some of these groups come from the Czech Republic. They wear typical white coats with white trousers; by contrast, the "Hungarian" infantry wore coloured trousers, and coats with pointed cuffs. Regiments could only be identified by the colours of the turnbacks, piping and buttons.

Headdress for Grenadiers was a fur cap with a brass front plate, the design of which changed more than once, finally being replaced by a simple grenade badge. Fusiliers - in Austrian parlance the infantry of the Line, rather than Light infantrymen - wore a leather helmet with a yellow and black woollen crest. A shako was introduced in 1806, but even in 1809 Fusiliers wore both types of headgear side by side. The equipment was of the normal European style, with only the Grenadiers carrying a sabre.

The Jägers were part of the Light infantry, and under the 1808 reorganisation were grouped in battalions of six

Austrian Grenadiers are easily recognized by their fur caps with the characteristic high front. The brass plate went through a number of changes over the years, and varied in detail from regiment to regiment, but always featured the coat of arms, the sovereign's cypher and various trophies. On the right side was worn the national pompon in yellow wool with a black centre. The different regiments were distinguished by the colours of their facings and buttons.

companies each. The regulations tied the Jägers to much more rigid tactical control than in other European armies; they had only limited freedom for skirmishing, which was regarded by the high command as of marginal value. Only a limited number of Jägers were armed with rifled *Stutzen,* about two-thirds of the personnel carrying smoothbore carbines. The *Stutzenjäger* carried a special sidearm: to compensate for the relatively short rifle their sword-bayonet was extra long, to give them a chance in close combat.

Jäger uniform was completely different from that of the Line infantry. The basic colour of coat and trousers was so-called "pike grey" with grass green collar, cuffs and piping. Headdress was a "Corsican" hat with a broad, partly up-turned brim, decorated with a goose-feather hackle and a yellow and black woollen pompon; officers wore cock feathers and more elaborate plumes. All leather equipment was black; more details are described in the photograph captions.

(Above) To identify a regiment by the colour is not easy, as various units wore nearly identical facings. It is easier to recognize the Austrian army's "German" infantry from its "Hungarian" regiments. This is a German unit, with Grenadiers in the foreground. Hungarian units wore coloured trousers with braiding on the thighs, and had pointed "Polish" coat cuffs.

(Left) Fusiliers and Grenadiers of a German infantry regiment. Fusiliers formed the centre or battalion companies in the Austrian army; from 1798 onwards they wore a black leather helmet with black and yellow wool crest and brass decorations, until this was replaced by a shako from 1809. The Fusiliers' only sidearm was the bayonet, only Grenadiers being issued with sabres. (Photo: Peter J. Nachtigall)

(Above) Fusiliers of a German infantry regiment, with light blue facings, wearing the 1809 pattern shako. German regiments wore white trousers with knee-high black cloth gaiters.

(Right) Historically Austria had always raised Jäger units on a "free corps" basis for the duration of any war; the first regular Jäger battalions were only formed in 1808. They were divided into short rifle (Stutzen) and carbine (Karabiner) Jägers, the former with Model 1798 rifles and the latter with shortened smoothbore muskets. Their grey tunics were worn with grey knee breeches and high black gaiters or white linen trousers.

(Above left) Carbine Jäger loading his weapon. This so-called "Corsican" felt hat, trimmed in leather for enlisted ranks, was also worn by Austrian specialist and technical troops. The wool pompon was always in the national colours of yellow and black; the green hackle for enlisted men was of goose feathers, officers wearing cocks' feathers.

(Left) The "Prima Plana" or senior NCO ranks equivalent to sergeant carried a special sabre with a decorated hilt. All NCOs had the yellow and black sword knot.

(Above) To protect the lock of the short rifle a special leather rain cover was issued, black like all other leather equipment and proofed with shellac. The equipment of the short rifle Jäger differed somewhat from his carbine-armed comrade; he carried a combination ramrod/loading hammer fixed to the crossbelt with a thong and D-rings. This Oberjäger's rank is indicated by his sabre and knot, gloves, and elaborate hat pompon bearing the royal cypher; his cane is invisible from this angle.

(Right) The equipment of a Oberjäger spread out on his greatcoat, which was rolled and strapped on to the knapsack for the march. He possesses a spare shirt, socks and underwear. The leather gloves are a sign of rank. His plate and spoon are made of wood, the cup of tin. The special Prima Plana sabre with the NCO sword knot is carried from a black crossbelt; and lying left of it, under the haversack, is his sergeant's cane of Spanish reed. The canteen is of the typical Csutora model, holding about 0.75 litre. The powderhorn hung on the right hip. The knapsack, though small, had an internal flap compartment for the hatchet. His personal belongings include writing, washing, cleaning and smoking kit. Flint and steel are stored with some tinder in a small bag; he also has a bottle-opener, and dice made from musket balls. On his haversack are displayed the pricker and brush for cleaning his lock, and a whistle, all with safety chains.

(Above) The extremely long
sword bayonet for the 1798 short
rifle was only issued for field
operations. It had to be carried
permanently fixed, as no
scabbard was issued; and while it
gave a vital increase in reach for
hand-to-hand fighting it
obviously destroyed the balance
of what was supposed to be a
precision firearm. Note also the
NCO's hat pompon with "FJ"
cypher, and the Spanish reed
cane.

(Left) In the ammunition pouch
a combination tool was usually
carried; Napoleonic soldiers
were definitely not encouraged to
disassemble their weapons, but
they had to be able to change a
flint or loosen off major
components for cleaning. Spare
flints were carried in the thin
leather pocket in the front.

(Above) The Jäger uniform was of "pike grey" with grass green facings. Underneath the coat, with its single row of yellow metal buttons, a grey waistcoat was worn. This Jäger cleaning his short rifle in camp is wearing the field cap or "woods cap".

(Right top & bottom) The raising of militia in Austria from 1808 produced six battalions of volunteers from Vienna, who fought in 1809 shoulder to shoulder with the regular units. This corporal wears the typical uniform of dark grey with red facings. The black leather equipment was standard infantry issue. He is armed with a Grenadier sabre decorated with the NCO sword knot; but in contrast to the sergeant he carries a hazel stick. The brass plate on his Corsican hat is engraved with the battalion number and "Wiener Freywillige".

British & Allied Troops

Many Continental states were, for different periods and with widely varying degrees of enthusiasm, engaged in coalitions with France which often involved providing troops for Napoleon's campaigns; but for nearly 20 years Britain was his most relentless opponent. The Royal Navy protected the British Isles from French invasion; as the shifting Continental alliances came and went Britain continually provided gold, weapons and intelligence assistance to any nation which would take up arms against the "Corsican ogre". While her navy was supreme, Britain's army started the wars with Revolutionary France in the 1790s with a poor reputation. Over nearly two decades, in numerous minor expeditions around the shores of Europe and further afield, and in major campaigns in Egypt, on the Spanish peninsula and in Central Europe, that army evolved once more into a battle-proven and professionally-led force able to face the best in the world with confidence. Among a number of brilliant officers perhaps the most important to this process was Arthur Wellesley, 1st Duke of Wellington.

For detailed historical information on those troops, and on the living history enthusiasts who recreate them today, see the accompanying Windrow & Greene title *"Wellington's Army Recreated in Colour Photographs"* by Neil Leonard, where the interested reader will find references to many infantry, cavalry and artillery re-enactment groups throughout Britain (and elsewhere - Canadian groups, known for their high quality, sometimes cross the Atlantic to thicken up Wellington's battle-line). Here we can give space only to a brief mention of a few units, encountered serving alongside German re-enactors at major Continental events, to represent the redcoats who at various dates confronted Napoleon and his allies.

The British infantry consisted during the Napoleonic Wars of a maximum of 104 Regiments of Foot and Light Infantry, entirely raised by voluntary enlistment - there was no conscription for the British army. These were numbered sequentially, in order of raising, most units also bearing a territorial name, but recruiting was not limited to that region. Regimental strength varied from one to four battalions; the battalion was the tactical unit, the regiment being largely an administrative identity. On campaign separate battalions from various regiments were formed into brigades. A battalion consisted normally of ten companies: one Grenadier and one Light company on the flanks, and eight Battalion or centre companies.

The British infantryman wore a red coatee, his regiment being distinguished by the particular combination of coloured collar, cuff and shoulderstrap facings and of woollen lace "loops" and edging applied to the coat. Before 1812 he wore a "stovepipe" shako, initially of

(Above) This member of the recreated Grenadier Company, 3rd Battalion, 1st Foot Guards wears the "Belgic" shako introduced in 1812, with a false front higher than the body, and a universal pattern of brass plate bearing the king's "GR" cypher.

leather but later of felt, with brass front plate and woollen tuft; from that date a new pattern appeared, with a felt false front taller than the body and new decorations including a tasselled cord; both types of shako were often protected in the field by an oilcloth cover. Campaign trousers were of grey woollen cloth, or of lighter white linen in hot climates, worn with short black canvas gaiters and shoes; for full dress tighter white trousers were worn with knee-length black gaiters. Grey greatcoats with caped shoulders were issued.

The equipment of the redcoat was very similar to that of the Continental soldier, comprising whitened crossbelts supporting the cartridge pouch and bayonet for his smoothbore flintlock musket ("Brown Bess"); sergeants carried a sword, and in centre companies a half-pike. The so-called "camp necessaries" issued for campaign included a haversack for rations, a heavy wooden water canteen, and the Trotter knapsack of tarred canvas.

Allied contingents

Apart from the German-speaking armies, many other forces fought alongside the British at one stage or another of the Napoleonic Wars; but these are regrettably not well represented in this book. The most obvious is the Russian army, which played such an

(**Above**) British Line and Light Infantry form a square during the 180th anniversary of the battle of Waterloo - an excellent defensive formation against cavalry attack, but horribly vulnerable to artillery. The standard of uniform and drill among the British Napoleonic re-enactment groups is often very high, as they have been in existence for several years longer than their German counterparts.

(**Right**) Re-enactors of the 68th Durham Light Infantry wearing the "stovepipe" pattern shako in use by all British infantry 1806-1812, and retained by Light and Rifles units thereafter when the Line adopted the Belgic type. Other distinctions of Light troops were the buglehorn shako insignia, the green tuft, and the fringed "wings" on the shoulders. The jacket facing colours, together with the coloured lines in the white woollen lace trim, were specific regimental identification features.

important part in the destruction the French 1st Empire, but which is missing from these pages. This is not because of any lack of re-enactment groups; for instance, the Pavlovski Grenadiers and the Kiev Line Grenadiers are just two of the groups now active in Russia on a very professional level, and regular events take place at Borodino and other historic sites. It is simply a matter of the distance and the cost of travelling to events in Western Europe which makes them infrequent guests at our re-enactments.

*   *   *

One other contingent with a varied history were the troops of today's Netherlands. Partly under Spanish/Austrian Hapsburg rule and partly independent, the Low Countries were occupied by the French early in the period. After Napoleon's first abdication a new independent Dutch-Belgian kingdom was created, and during the Hundred Days in 1815 Dutch and Belgian troops fought on the Allied side, with variable enthusiasm and success - but despite British prejudice, contemporary records show that many units fought gallantly at Quatre Bras and Waterloo. Dutch re-enactors may be found at all the larger events in Europe.

(Above) British officers were identifiable by the crimson silk net waist sash and the sword. The design and materials of their uniforms were finer than for enlisted men, the colours brighter, the tailoring smarter, and the lacing and other embellishments of silver or gold wire braid. These three neatly display three different ways of wearing the laced lapels of the coatee - buttoned right across, buttoned partly back to show the lacing at the top, and buttoned completely back.

(Above right) Infantry drummers wore special tunics with elaborate braiding, as here displayed by the drummer of the recreated 3/1st Foot Guards. The drum was used to transmit orders on the battlefield and also to keep the rhythm on the march; each Line company had a drummer, who before c.1812 wore a jacket in reversed colours - i.e. in the facing colour of his regiment, faced with red.

(Right) The British army's equivalent of the German Jäger units were the two Rifle regiments - the 60th and 95th - raised from 1800, armed with Baker rifles, and highly trained in light infantry tactics. The 95th, recreated here, wore dark green uniforms with black collars, cuffs and shoulderstraps piped white.

(**Above & left**) With their knapsacks laid aside and with bayonets fixed, the 68th Durham Light Infantry manoeuvre on the battlefield of Waterloo, authentically muddy for the 1995 re-enactment.

(Above) Roll-call of the redcoats - a striking scene from the Waterloo event. After the battle sergeants would call the nominal roll of their companies, passing to their officers lists of the dead, wounded and missing.

(Right) Officers and men of different units regroup following the 1995 Waterloo re-enactment - here the difference in pattern between a battalion's Regimental and King's Colours is clearly seen (although in this case they are of different regiments). In battle the ensigns carrying the colours would be guarded by half-a-dozen selected sergeants, usually armed with half-pikes; as in every army, the loss of the colours was the greatest shame any unit could suffer,and men frequently died in their defence.

(Above) Troopers of the 12th (Prince of Wales's) Light Dragoons wait behind the British infantry lines. The cavalryman had to carry nearly all his belongings in the cylindrical valise behind the saddle. The sheepskin saddle cover gave some degree of comfort during long hours of riding.

(Left) Smart in dark blue faced with yellow, a horseman of the 12th Light Dragoons gallops through the Allied artillery back to his regiment's position on Mont St.Jean. His shabraque bears the royal cypher below the Prince of Wales's Feathers, and the abbreviated regimental name and number are displayed on the ends of his valise.

(Above) England has some first class cavalry re-enactment groups, and during living history events rules very similar to real campaign life apply: the trooper's first care is always for his horse. Here a man of the 12th Light Dragoons saddles his horse after a night in bivouac - note the authentic stable dress.

(Above right & right) Men of the 15th (King's) Light Dragoons (Hussars) at Waterloo, with the red felt shako worn by this regiment from 1812 both displayed and in its oilskin cover. The light cavalry's tasks were reconaissance, screening of advances and retreats, raids, and also charges as part of formed cavalry brigades in pitched battle.

(**Left**) An officer of the 15th Hussars protects himself with a long blue coat against the wind and rain during the march of the Prussian Brigade before the official 1995 Waterloo spectacle.

(**Below left**) The number of Dutch-Belgian troops fighting on the Allied side at Waterloo was nearly as high as the British; unfortunately this is not reflected in today's re-enactment scene, although there are a number of good Dutch-Belgian units. These two troopers belong to the 2nd Belgian Carabiniers, and display typical heavy cavalry uniform and long thrusting swords.

(**Below right**) Following the reorganisation of the Dutch-Belgian army the 16th Infantry Regiment was granted in 1815 the title of Jagers. Their coat became green with yellow facings and they wore black leather equipment; all other items were of standard infantry pattern. In camp a field cap was worn, replaced for full dress by a shako of Austrian pattern with an orange cockade. He is armed with the French 1777 musket; note, from this angle, the buttstock slightly off-set to the right to allow the eye to come more easily into line with the barrel when firing from the shoulder.

42nd Royal Highland Regiment

The recreated "Black Watch" is not really a German re-enactment group, but it has to be mentioned here as the only German-based group that brings Wellington's redcoats back to life. The 42nd Regiment's section in Germany, formed in 1989, includes British, American, Canadian and Australian re-enactors. The popularity of the Highland soldier stems from the historical reputation of Britain's Scottish troops - always steady and reliable, and distinguished by extraordinary bravery on scores of battlefields. During the Napoleonic period these regiments retained their local roots in particular areas of Scotland, and thus enjoyed particularly strong *esprit de corps*.

The Black Watch was raised in 1739 as the 43rd Regiment of Foot from six independent local security companies (thus "Watch"), being the first Highland unit in the British army; the "Black" is believed to have referred to their dark tartan. In 1749 they were renumbered as the 42nd Highland Regiment of Foot, being granted the title "Royal" for their record in the French/Indian Wars in North America; and many other overseas postings followed. During the Napoleonic Wars the 42nd distinguished themselves in Egypt and the Peninsula, culminating in their heroism as part of Picton's 5th Division at Quatre Bras and Waterloo, where they were one of only four regiments individually mentioned by the Duke of Wellington in his account of the battle.

The peculiarities of the Highland uniform make extra demands upon re-enactors. The coatee, though slightly shorter than the English type, was generally similar. The traditional kilt was still usually worn in the field, a length of heavy, pleated cloth in the regimental ("government") pattern of tartan wrapped and belted around the body. (On campaign, for practical reasons, standard army trousers or "trews" made up in regimental tartan might sometimes be substituted). Checkered wool stockings were worn with canvas gaiters and shoes. The headdress was the Kilmarnock bonnet in blue wool with a characteristic chequered headband, with a cockade and regimental badge; depending upon availability, the bonnet was "mounted" all round with falling black ostrich feather plumes. With certain unit differences the soldier's equipment and armament were the same as for the rest of the Line.

(**Above**) The bonnet of the 42nd had a band chequered white, red and green. The leather visor was only worn in the field, so was temporarily tied in place. The black ostrich feathers often gave reason for complaint: sometimes the men wore them in exaggeratedly large bunches; at other times the wear and tear of campaigning reduced them to only one or two bedraggled feathers per bonnet. The design of the British crossbelt plate varied from regiment to regiment.

(**Above right**) There was not much difference between the equipment of a Highland soldier and his English comrade. To stow his belongings he had the Trotter knapsack, successor of the envelope knapsack; it was usually tarred black but other colours might also be found; nearly all units painted the knapsacks with their number or insignia. Strapped to it was a blanket or greatcoat. A minimum of spare clothing was carried; peculiar to the Scottish units might be trews - trousers made up from tartan kilt material, here of the 42nd's "government" sett. The forage cap has a red tourie or tuft. The canteen, haversack and D-section messtin are standard issue, as are the bayonet and its crossbelt closed by the regimental pattern plate, and the cartridge pouch, though its plate is a unit peculiarity. His private belongings are limited to eating, writing and smoking kit, cards and dice, flint and steel.

(**Right**) During the Napoleonic Wars the traditional Highland broadsword was carried only by sergeants and some officers; junior ranks had only the bayonet for their Brown Bess as a sidearm. The spontoon or half-pike carried by sergeants of Battalion and Grenadier companies was more a sign of rank than a weapon, but it was useful in hand-to-hand fighting around the colours. When wearing the kilt a sporran might be used; for the 42nd it was white with black tassels.

(Left) Sergeant of the Grenadier Company with his half-pike. The padded and fringed wings on the shoulders were the sign of the two flank companies of each Line battalion. The red and white hackle in the bonnet identifies the 42nd's Grenadiers; in other units the Grenadiers wore white tufts, the Battalion companies red and white, and Light companies green, but the 42nd's Battalion companies had been granted the right to a red hackle in 1801. The broadsword ceased being general issue and became a sergeant's distinction in 1776; in Highland units the standard sergeant's waist sash, in crimson with a centrestripe of facing colour, was worn over the left shoulder instead. Sergeants' lace jacket trim was plain white, not interwoven with coloured threads like that of the rank-and-file.

(Below & top right) The international Highland Brigade - with members from Britain, Germany, America and Australia - on the march during the 1995 Waterloo commemoration; and forming square. Their strength, together with the sound of the pipes and drums, gave them an impressive appearance beyond the reach of many re-enactment groups of equally high standard in dress and drill, but simply lacking manpower.

(Below right) Members of the Grenadier Company wore a grenade insignia on their bonnet cockade, instead of the sphinx badge granted to the regiment for gallantry in Egypt in 1801. Here they wear the white trousers used in some summer campaigns in the Peninsula. This is the only German-based re-enactment group recreating Wellington's redcoats; at international events they amalgamate with the other Highland groups.

Armament

The standard infantry weapon issued by all nations engaged in the Napoleonic Wars was a smoothbore flintlock musket. The system of ignition was essentially unchanged between c.1690 and c.1840, only details being modified. These alterations sometimes owed as much to the whim of a particular sovereign as to technical improvements. For instance, the buttstock of the old Prussian flintlock - known as the "calf-foot" - was shaped perfectly for smart drill movements but less conveniently for actual shooting. The Prussian 1788 instructions put more emphasis on drill than on marksmanship - understandably, given the limited likelihood of an individual soldier achieving a hit with an aimed shot from a flintlock smoothbore.

To make loading simpler and quicker, the diameter of the soft lead ball was made smaller than the inner diameter of the unrifled barrel (roughly .75 inch). This was necessary, as not all barrels had exactly the same calibre and also, after a number of shots, they started to "foul" with the burnt residue of the gunpowder. The difference between ball and barrel diameter was compensated for by the paper of the cartridge, a folded tube containing the powder charge of roughly one ounce, and the ball of similar weight. After pouring some powder from the cartridge into the external priming pan, and the rest down the barrel, the bullet and paper were inserted into the muzzle and pushed home with the ramrod.

Loading and firing the musket were practised repeatedly. The Prussian infantry of Friedrich the Great were able to fire five to six volleys per minute - a remarkable record, which can seldom if ever have been matched by any troops in 1813-15. The "Line" infantry usually advanced and fought drawn up in close-packed ranks, and fired at short range by modern standards - 50 to 100 yards; so careful aiming was not neccessary. This is the reason why nearly all muskets from this period have a small front sight (if any), but no rearsight: any serious attempt to aim would only have reduced the firing speed, individual hits were unlikely, and after each volley the powder smoke got thicker, soon blanking out even the massed target of an enemy battle-line.

Marksmanship training was therefore confined to Jägers and Riflemen armed with rifles - weapons with spiral grooving cut into the interior of the barrel, imparting a spin to the tighter-fitting ball and consequently sending it straighter over longer ranges. It was 1809 before target practice became a regular feature of Prussian infantry training. The results of an 1810 test with different contemporary weapons are summarised in the accompanying table; they demonstrate why only the massed volley of a body of troops could have a significant effect on the enemy.

To the limitations of accuracy were added those of reliability. Under battlefield conditions about every seventh shot would misfire. At best this required simply repriming the pan, or poking the touchhole clear of fouling with the brass pricker every man carried handy. Even a good flint - well-shaped, without flaws, and firmly screwed into the jaws of the cock - needed replacing after at most 50 shots. But if

(Above) Muzzle of a French Model 1777 musket. This ramrod, like most of its day, needed to be turned through 180 degrees after drawing from its pipes before the enlarged end was pushed down the bore. Socket bayonets were fixed by fitting an L-shaped slot over a lug and twisting to lock. The upper band, holding barrel and stock together, had a small brass foresight, but hardly any muskets were fitted with rearsights.

his powder was wet or otherwise unserviceable the soldier might have to unload the musket. Each man carried a corkscrew-shaped "worm" which could be screwed onto his ramrod; he would twist this until it engaged with the soft lead of the ball firmly enough for him to pull it out of the barrel, and after emptying out the paper and powder he was ready to reload the piece.

While the flintlock musket remained essentially unchanged for more than a century, minor improvments were tried. In 1773 Prussia adopted a cylindrical ramrod, the same section at both ends; previous models were narrower than the bore with a single swollen ramming end, so had to be reversed in the hand after withdrawing from their stowage under the barrel, and after use. The cylindrical ramrod saved a few seconds during the loading drill, at the cost of increased weight.

A more practical invention was the conical touch hole, forming a tiny funnel from inside the breech end of the barrel out into the priming pan. With the addition of a breechplug cut at an angle to form a ramp shape, this meant that when the main charge was rammed down the barrel some powder was automatically forced out the touchhole into the pan (which was closed by the frizzen). This eliminated the whole process of priming the pan from the cartridge, closing the frizzen, and then reversing the musket to load from the muzzle. Although this made a real difference to the loading time, a problem emerged: the touchhole tended to become enlarged with use, and the resulting pyrotechnics were dangerous to the next man in line to the right. An external fireshield was added around the pan.

A further step towards a genuinely "standardised" weapon was the French Model 1777 musket, slightly modified after

(Above) Flintlock action of a good reproduction French M1777 musket, later fitted with a priming pan shield for Prussian use. The lock was as solid and reliable as the whole design, which was widely copied in subsequent early 19th century Prussian, Russian and Austrian muskets.

the Revolution of 1789 and designated "Model 1777 (corrigé en l'an IX)". This musket had a very well-shaped stock and a reliable flintlock action with a strong cock (too light a cock often snapped at the neck with prolonged use). The barrel was fixed into the stock by three bands, a method making it easy to remove for cleaning. A degree of controlled mass production by factories, all parts being made to minimum tolerances, brought interchangeability of parts with only minor individual fitting - which had always been a problem with old Prussian arms, whose parts were made to generous tolerances. Captured French muskets became available to Prussia in large numbers after the Russian campaign, and were gratefully received by an army always short of weapons. The new muskets developed in Prussia, Austria and Russia at the beginning of the 19th century were clearly influenced by the French Model 1777.

Notwithstanding this war booty, and deliveries of weapons from Russia, Austria and England, the Prussian troops of 1813-15 suffered from a chronic shortage of firearms and edged weapons. During the disastrous defeats of 1806 large quantities of weapons were lost, damaged or destroyed. The "new Prussian" models - the 1809 musket and 1810 rifle - became available only in very small numbers, just enough to equip the Guards. The Line infantry, and especially the Landwehr, had a constant struggle with these deficiencies. It was impossible to equip a regiment with a single type of musket, although they tried to standardise at company or battalion level. In militia units even this was not possible, and for lack of muskets pikes were sometimes issued.

The shortage of firearms led to the establishment of factories in Berlin, Königsberg, Graudenz and Kolberg to assemble serviceable muskets from all available spare parts,

captured and damaged guns. The production of new firearms never reached sufficient numbers during the Wars of Liberation, because most factories had to be set up from scratch. Only the historic Potsdam arsenal delivered in quantity. The Neisse factory was instructed to deliver an annual total of 5,400 Model 1809 muskets. In the first year it managed only 500; in 1810, 2,000; and in 1811, 3,725 muskets plus 150 Model 1811 cavalry rifles. The Saarn and Danzig arsenals had similar problems.

The supply of edged weapons was also completely inadequate until years after the victory over Napoleon, and everything available was pressed into use - the old Prussian Model 1715 sabre, the new Prussian Model 1808, the captured French *sabre-briquet* which the latter copied, the Fusilier sidearm, and virtually any other kind of edged blade, not excluding hatchets.

Target practice results, 1810

The target was a panel 1.88m (approx.6 feet) high, by 31.4m (102 feet) long, thus representing a formed body of troops with a frontage of perhaps 50 men. At each of the four ranges 200 shots were fired. The numbers of hits anywhere in the panel, out of 200 shots, were listed as follows; these should therefore be halved for per centage hits:

Musket	at 75m	at 150m	at 225m	at 300m
"Old" Prussian M1780	92	64	64	42
M1780 modified	150	100	68	42
Nothardt M1805	145	97	56	67
"New" Prussian M1809	149	105	58	32
French M1777/1802	151	99	53	55
"Brown Bess"	94	116	75	55
Russian M1809	104	74	51	49

(**Right**) To polish the metal parts of weapons powdered brick and a few drops of oil from the bottle were mixed to make an abrasive; this was effective at removing rust but, if used over a matter of years, weakened the metal. The spring clamp was used when replacing broken springs from the flintlock (it was only issued to NCOs).

(**Below**) The leather cartridge pouches used by the various national armies almost invariably contained a snugly-fitting wooden block, differing only in minor details. This French block has compartments for packets of cartridges; others had holes drilled for individual cartridges. The metal tube contains oil. The brass loop shape is a "swab" tip to hold bits of rag for cleaning the bore; like the corkscrew-shaped "worm", it could be screwed to the end of the ramrod for use.

(Above) Muskets were loaded with paper cartridges. A strong piece of paper (thus our surviving term "cartridge paper") was cut to a specific size and formed into a tube by rolling round a wooden rod. One end was folded closed, and the soft lead ball was dropped in. A charge of black powder was measured out with a scoop and poured into the tube with a funnel; then the second end of the cartridge was folded closed. Today re-enactors make their own ammunition - obviously, without the bullet. In the Prussian army cartridges were only made by artillery depots and delivered to the units in bulk.

LOADING THE MUSKET

The following photographs demonstrate the difference between loading a smoothbore musket and a rifle.

(Right, above & below) In the Prussian and other armies loading was drilled again and again until every step could be performed automatically with speed and precision. After firing a volley reloading started immediately. Armed here with the modified French M1777

musket, a militiaman of the 5th Westphalian Landwehr Infantry is holding the musket in front of his body at the point of balance; he has pulled the cock back to half-cock (safety) position, and has roughly cleaned out the pan with his right thumb. Now he reaches for a cartridge from his pouch.

(Far left) The cartridge is brought to the mouth, and the folded "non-bullet end" is bitten off and spat out (surgeons always checked the state of recruits' teeth; and black powder battlefields were covered with bits of torn paper).

(Centre left) A small amount of powder is poured into the priming pan, and the spring-loaded frizzen is snapped closed to retain it.

(Left) The musket butt is placed on the ground, and the remaining powder poured down the muzzle, followed by the ball still in its paper wrapping. The ramrod is taken from its place under the barrel, reversed, and the wide end used to tamp the ball and paper firmly down onto the powder charge; then the ramrod must be replaced in its groove or tubes.

(Below left) On the command "Ready!" the cock is pulled back to full-cock position; at the command "Level!" the firing position is adopted. On the command "Fire!" the trigger is pulled; the flint knocks the frizzen forward off the pan and simultaneously strikes sparks into the priming. This flares up, and after an appreciable moment of "hang fire" the sparks passing through the touchhole from pan into barrel set off the main charge. The soldier then automatically goes into his reloading drill. Note the effect of the Prussian pan shield: sparks and flame from the priming fly upwards only, not outwards into the face of the man next right in line.

LOADING THE RIFLE
Loading a rifle for a precisely aimed shot was more difficult and time-consuming. The ball had to grip into the spiral rifling grooves inside the barrel, and so had to fit snugly into the bore without the musket's 1-2mm "windage". The process is demonstrated here by a member of the 2nd Light Bn., KGL, with a Baker rifle.

(Right) First the rifleman has to fill a powder measure with an exact amount released by the spring nozzle of his powderhorn.

(Left) The powder is poured into the muzzle.

(Below) From the patch box in the buttstock he has already taken a patch, and chewed it soft. He takes a loose ball from the small pouch on his belt, centres it on the patch in the muzzle, and starts it on its way with gentle taps of the loading mallet.

(Above left) The handle of the mallet has the same diameter as the bore, and is used to push the bullet deeper into the barrel.

(Above right) Now, with the rifle firmly held between the knees, he pulls the ramrod from its pipes, takes it with both hands, and rams the bullet all the way down. This needs some strength, and becomes more difficult after every shot as the bore becomes increasingly fouled with burnt powder. The Prussian Jägers actually carried bullets in up to 12 different diameters to counter this problem, using progressively smaller balls as firing went on.

(Right) The ramrod is replaced in its stowage; and the priming pan is filled with powder from the horn.

(**Above**) The weapon is cocked, and ready to fire. Provided that the loading was efficient, the powder dry and unseparated, the touchhole unobstructed, and the flint unflawed and firm in the jaws, the rifle should discharge...

(**Right**)...though occasionally with alarming consequences. The Baker did not have the pan shield fitted to Prussian smoothbore muskets.

Artillery

The recreation of historical artillery batteries is a huge undertaking. The cost of a single Napoleonic uniform and equipment can reach a thousand pounds; for a group to club together to raise the several thousand additional pounds needed for the construction of an accurate, firing cannon demands serious dedication. A few years ago reduced size replicas were a common sight, but today scale accuracy is demanded. While it is well established in the United States, and several artillery groups exist in Great Britain, this branch of re-enactment is in its infancy in Germany. However, some Napoleonic groups are working on the construction of guns, and within a season or two we may hope to hear the roar of artillery more frequently on the historic battlefields of Central Europe.

The photographs on the following pages should therefore be seen only as representative, hinting at the attraction of a good artillery demonstration. The only German group is the Grossherzoglich-Hessische-Feldartillerie-Korps. The original unit from Hesse-Darmstadt served with the forces of the Confederation of the Rhine, organised and equipped like the French artillery. This unit fought with distinction in several campaigns; they even survived the retreat from Russia in excellent order, with the transport train intact and only one gun lost.

To even summarise the technical and organisational differences between the artillery arms of only the major

(**Above**) Striking photograph of a French gun crew in action early in a battle recreation. Although only a few cannon rounds have yet been fired the powder smoke has already laid a thick fog over the battlefield. Given that the numbers of re-enactors firing here are only a tiny fraction of the number of soldiers who actually fought in Napoleonic actions, this picture gives an idea of the visibility during a black powder battle on a still day. Historical accounts of regiments being surprised by sudden attacks, even over open ground, become much easier to understand.

combatant armies would be well beyond the size of this book. Most interesting for the re-enactment scene is the field artillery. This branch used guns light enough to accompany the infantry on campaign, pulled by teams of between four and 12 horses. They were used against enemy strongpoints or formed bodies of troops. Skilfull use of massed batteries could break up and weaken the enemy line in preparation for infantry or cavalry attacks, or blunt and disrupt an enemy attack before its impetus fell on the defending battle-line.

Field artillery pieces were termed either "guns" - longer- barrelled pieces, used in direct fire with a straight trajectory; or "howitzers" - shorter-barrelled pieces used for lobbing projectiles at a high angle, to reach targets behind cover or crests. They were sometimes fielded separately, sometimes in mixed batteries with one or two howitzers to half a dozen guns. Artillery was classified by the weight of the ball in pounds (for guns), or sometimes by the measured calibre (for howitzers). Field guns used iron balls, howitzers often stone ones; thus a howitzer ball of the same weight as a field gun ball would have a much larger diameter. As there was no international standardisation in weights and measures,

"one pound" weight did not mean the same everywhere, and artillery could seldom make use of captured enemy ammunition. The standard weights used by all European nations varied between 3lbs. and 12lbs.; light "3-pounder" and "4-pounder" pieces were still used in some Continental armies as "battalion guns" directly attached in ones and twos to infantry units.

The kinds of guns in use, and their transport and supply trains, varied in detail but were essentially similar in all armies. The French led in artillery design, their standardised Gribeauval system giving a high degree of commonality; e.g., a gun wheel damaged in battle could be replaced on the spot with a wheel from an artillery wagon. The Gribeauval system was also used by some French satellite armies.

The type of ammunition mainly used in guns was roundshot, a solid iron ball effective against both "soft" and "hard" targets. Contemporary sources state that these balls, normally never fired at more than a man's height above the ground, cut bloody aisles in enemy columns. Also available for use in howitzers were shells - hollow balls filled with gunpowder; these were detonated by a time fuze ignited by the propellant charge, in theory exploding on arrival. However, the correct calculation of range and cutting of the fuze to an appropriate length was difficult in the heat of battle. Shrapnel shells ("spherical case") were invented by the British and only available to them and to the German contingents equipped by them, e.g. the KGL artillery; these were round shells filled with musket balls and a small bursting charge, which could be

(Above left) The Hesse-Darmstadt artillery re-enactment group wear uniforms of the 1809 period; their predecessors fought in this gear as part of the Confederation of the Rhine with Napoleon against Austria. This cut of coat was typical for Hesse-Darmstadt units, though colour, facings, piping and lacing varied from regiment to regiment - the artillery wore dark blue with black facings, piped red. In camp a French style undress cap was worn. Clearly visible are the small central fly flap on the early trousers, and the waistcoat worn underneath the coat.

(Above) The enlisted man's shako has a leather chinstrap and a pompon in regimental colour - feather hackles were also worn.

fired from both guns and howitzers to burst in the air above the enemy.

Most devastating against infantry and cavalry at short range was canister shot, a cylindrical tin container holding dozens of musket balls. When the gun or howitzer was fired the canister tore open in the barrel, leaving the balls to travel on in a cone-shaped pattern like the discharge of a giant shotgun. For defence against massed attacks at short range it was common to load a piece with both a roundshot and canister, which could do appalling damage.

(Above left) The French pattern shako of this corporal has the red and white pompon and white metal chinscales of his rank. The cockade is in the Hessian colours of red and white.

(Above) The linstock with slowmatch was used to set fire to the priming tube (usually a quill filled with powder and inserted in the touchhole). Note the corporal's shoulderstraps piped in silver.

(Left) This howitzer is a light piece, as previously used by Hessian troops during the American War of Independence. The cartridge pouch flap of the corporal is covered with white linen, bearing the cypher "L" for Ludwig; and he wears French-style sleeve insignia of rank.

(Above) Wearing a leather thumb stall, one man blocks the air flow through the touchhole (which might fan a dying spark into life) as another rams home the next round; the swabber has just cleaned the bore with a wet sponge to douse any smouldering debris from the previous shot, but every precaution is still taken. The wooden boxes each side of the barrel carried some "immediate use" charges, while most of the ammunition was stored in special wagons kept well back from the gun line. The re-enactor on the left wears a *bricole*, a crossbelt with a rope used to manhandle the piece. The veteran on the right still wears the old pattern pre-1800 coat; it was not uncommon to use up existing stocks as long as they lasted, especially on campaign.

(Above right) After loading the howitzer and checking direction and elevation, the linstock is applied to the priming tube, leading directly into the ready-pierced bag of the previously prepared powder charge.

(Right) French Artillery of the Imperial Guard, recreated by a British group, get their instructions for the 1993 anniversary of the Battle of the Nations at Leipzig from a Prussian captain of the Engineer Corps. The re-enactment hobby knows no national frontiers.

(Opposite top) Life-size artillery pieces are very expensive; their brute weight can cause transportation problems; the safety aspect can embroil re-enactors in bureaucratic and legal complications - but once on the battlefield, there is little that can match their sinister majesty. Here a Nassau unit prepare their gun at Waterloo in 1995.

(Opposite below) The split second before detonation of the main charge. The crew, uniformed as Dutch horse gunners, are at a safe distance to avoid the recoil of the piece.

(Left) The French Guard Artillery fire their 12-pounder Gribeauval field gun against advancing Prussian troops at Leipzig. The artillery were often the target for skirmishers and sudden cavalry attacks. A momentarily seized enemy gun did not have to be dragged off; to disable a cannon it was enough to hammer a headless soft iron spike into the touchhole.

(Below) A Dutch foot battery firing their gun. In the background is the reduced scale model of the farmhouse of La Haye Sainte as it is set up for the Waterloo anniversaries. (The trail axle at left foreground is not a period item, but a practical tool for manoeuvring the heavy gun.)

France

" *Vive l'Empéreur"* is heard as a greeting among German re-enactors as often as *"Es lebe der König"*. Alongside the recreated German units, the Napoleonische Gesellschaft includes a regiment of *Infanterie de Ligne*, a *Demi-Brigade* formed from Revolutionary War *Volontaires,* and representatives of the Emperor's artillery and *Grenadiers* and *Chasseurs de la Garde Impériale*. The dramatic, and for many years victorious history of the armies of the Republic, the Consulate and the 1st Empire has an appeal to military history enthusiasts of all nations, and Germany is no exception. The few pages which follow offer only a representative example of this activity; and these notes can only hint at the richness and diversity of the subject (to be covered in more depth in at least two forthcoming books in this series).

The French Revolution of 1789 brought dramatic changes to the military structures of the "old regime". The old system of named regiments was abolished; and in 1791 the raising of numerous volunteer and conscript battalions began, as the infant Republic faced determined attempts by the old powers of Europe to strangle this dangerous newcomer. This *levée en masse* naturally created units of widely varying quality.

Patchily equipped, virtually untrained, and with inexperienced leadership, the new battalions could not operate according to the difficult linear tactics in which the old professional army had been painstakingly instructed. Even simple manoeuvres in formed units were beyond their abilities, leading to dislocation and confusion. To cope with this problem urgently, the French authorities began to form "half-brigades" based on pre-Revolutionary units. Each regular battalion was backed up by two of the newly raised battalions, the old unit forming the centre as the 2nd Battalion, with the young troops of the 1st and 3rd Battalions forming the flanks. The reliably drilled and trained centre could thus develop its firepower in a linear formation, with the flanks advancing in columns to gain ground. These dense, simple formations relying upon mass impetus suited the enthusiastic but unskilled recruits. This basic approach - though greatly refined by a commander of genius, and incorporating co-ordinated support from skirmishing light infantry, artillery and cavalry - was the cornerstone of all French conquests for the next 20 years.

In 1803 the Demi-Brigades were retitled as numbered regiments of Line or Light Infantry, the term half-brigade being retained only for tactical groupings of various battalions. There was little difference between the uniforms, and none between the weapons of the Line and Light units; though the latter might be sent forward of the main battle-line as skirmishers, they might equally fight in line and column. Each battalion had a heavy and a light company, termed Grenadiers and Voltigeurs in the Line units, forming on the flanks of the Fusiliers of the centre companies.

Due to the system of mass conscription, which continued throughout the Napoleonic period, the French infantry were

This German group recreates the Grenadier Company of the 1er Bataillon des Gardes Nationales Volontaires du Haut-Rhin, recruited in Alsace in 1791. Ambitiously, they plan to follow the development of their chosen unit through the whole period up to 1815, shadowing the historical changes in identity, uniform and organisation exactly 200 years later. This patriot of the mid-1790s wears the 1793 coat, with the red epaulettes distinguishing Grenadiers.

very numerous. The branches which required more extensive training and more costly equipment - the artillery, cavalry and technical troops - were also greatly expanded over the years, but could not increase their numbers as quickly as the infantry mass. In addition to the regular line Napoleon built up his Imperial Guard as an élite reserve; initially, at least, these expensively equipped and better paid regiments were drawn from carefully selected veterans of line units, though by 1813-15 casualties and less discriminating enlistment had somewhat diluted their quality.

French army uniforms of the period are an immensely complex field of study. There were numerous branches of service, with internal distinctions of unit, rank and appointment; the army was born from the re-organised forces of the old regime mixed with new and hastily raised Revolutionary units; supplies of all sorts were often limited, uneven and regional; local manufature to less than rigid patterns was common; and the individuality of the French character found frequent and arbitrary expression.

(Above & opposite) By 1796 the former Volunteer National Guard of the Upper Rhine had evolved into the 102e Demi-Brigade de Ligne, but their recreators still give a striking impression of the typically motley French Revolutionary armies. In the years following the Revolution everything was in short supply and uniformity was low on the agenda. In the photo opposite three different greatcoats may be observed. The fur-trimmed 1791 leather helmet was not much liked by the troops, who preferred the more comfortable bicorn.

(Right) "En avant!" - the battles of the 1790s were often decided by a massed bayonet charge in column formation. Often the coat was the only more-or-less uniform item worn - if that. The foreground soldier wears the *veste* as an undress uniform jacket, with trousers of matress ticking material. Bicorns bore cockades and a variety of plumes and tufts in the colours of the young republic.

(Above) Revolutionary France was as short of sidearms as Prussia would be 20 years later, and at first only NC0s were to receive sabres; this sergeant (right - his gold cuff stripe is just visible) has managed to obtain a Sapper's pattern sabre. He also has one of the many varieties of privately acquired water-bottle - there was no regulation issue. Unit drummer boys (left) were often recruited from local orphanages.

(Left) Camp sentry in the chilly dawn; he wears a Prussian "booty" watchcoat, made up from blanket material. These tents are made to historical specifications.

(Above right) For volley firing a line was formed two ranks deep; under French regulations the first rank could kneel with the second rank firing over their heads.

(Right) Voltigeurs of the 9e Demi-Brigade Légère, c.1802; note the number painted on the shako cover.

(Far right) A pensive corporal of Grenadiers; again, such details as waistcoats and trousers varied considerably in the Revolutionary armies.

(Above) The equipment of a French infantryman - presumably an NCO, since he carries a copy of the 1791 regulations. Apart from small-clothes and typical personal belongings, washing kit, weapons accessories, etc., French troops often carried a *sac à distribution* - a large bag, convenient for carrying the fruits of looting and requisition. A spare pair of shoes were a luxury; contemporary reports often describe soldiers fighting barefoot. The white woollen sleeved waistcoat, here with red collar and cuffs, could be worn as undress uniform or under the coat for warmth. The white linen trousers and gaiters were normally stored in the knapsack to protect them on dirty marches. Beside the undress cap - *bonnet de police* - is a simple red night cap.

(Left) *Sapeur* (pioneer) of the Foot Grenadiers of the Imperial Guard, distinguished by his regulation beard, his sleeve insignia, and the absence of a brass front plate from his bearskin cap.

(Right) Members of the recreated Grenadier Company of the 111th Line Infantry Regiment, displaying the red distinctions of their status. The enlisted men wear the 1810 shako plate while the senior NCO at left still has the 1806 pattern.

(Above) The light or Voltigeur Company of an infantry regiment were often detached to skirmish ahead, to engage the enemy first and cause casualties and disruption in his ranks before the main clash of forces. These French skirmishers, in the 1812 uniform, are led by an officer distinguished by his gold-laced shako, his gorget and his sword.

(Left) Chasseurs of a Light Infantry Regiment - identifiable by their blue trousers, yellow and green distinctions, and the buglehorn pouch flap badge - carry a wounded comrade from the field using their muskets as an improvised stretcher.

(Above right) Grenadiers of Line and Guard regiments charging the Allied forces on Mont St.Jean during the 1995 Waterloo commemoration. For safety reasons re-enactors are not supposed to fix bayonets during close encounters, but this regulation is not invariably respected. Under provocation it is not entirely unknown for British troops to be ordered to fix bayonets in turn; the cold rattle of a large unit obeying this order simultaneously may have a sobering effect, restoring common sense all round.

(Right) The red fringed epaulettes distinguish this naval gunner as a senior NCO; corporals wore unfringed contre-epaulettes, and enlisted men simple shoulderstraps. The shako plate is of 1812 pattern, a period when naval artillery regiments were already well established in the shore role; the blockading of much of France's fleet during the latter years of the Napoleonic Wars made it pointless to leave trained gun crews idle in port.

(Far right) For re-enacted battles the British cavalrymen of the 12th Light Dragoons sometimes adopt the *czapka* and the lance, and modify their uniforms, to give a rough impression of Napoleon's Polish lancers of the Vistula Legion, who also wore dark blue faced with yellow.

(Above) During the 1995 Waterloo re-enactment British 15th Hussars clash with French 7th Hussars and 1st Mounted Chasseurs.
(Photo: Peter J.Nachtigall)

(Right) A handsomely mounted French cavalry officer, his cloak apparently hiding the finery of the Mounted Chasseurs of the Imperial Guard, who accompanied the historic march of the Prussian Brigade and their British cavalry escort before the 1995 Waterloo event.

(Above & above right) Splendid recreation of the French 7th Hussars, complete with bearskin busby, fur-trimmed pelisse, braided dolman, barrel sash and buttoned campaign overalls; his weapon is the 1786 hussar pattern sabre.

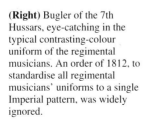

(Right) Bugler of the 7th Hussars, eye-catching in the typical contrasting-colour uniform of the regimental musicians. An order of 1812, to standardise all regimental musicians' uniforms to a single Imperial pattern, was widely ignored.

(Opposite top) One of the missions of the light horse was to raid behind enemy lines and interdict communications; and before the 1995 Waterloo commemoration these energetic French hussars nearly changed the course of re-enacted history when they intercepted "General von Blücher" on the road during the historic march of the Prussian Brigade.... Could the presence of that lone Chasseur officer (page 92) have had anything to do with this?

(Opposite below left) A senior NCO of the 1st Cuirassiers, representing the heavy cavalry divisions which played such a gallant part at Waterloo in 1815, riding up the slope of Mont St.Jean again and again, to smash themselves against the rocks of the Allied infantry squares.

(Opposite below right) A recreated trooper of another legendary Waterloo cavalry regiment - the Dutch-raised 2nd Lancers of the Imperial Guard, the immortal "Red Lancers".

(Overleaf) A magnificently uniformed staff officer, his red and gold brassard identifying him as an aide-de-camp to a *Général de Division*.

(Above & right) A trooper of the recreated 1st Mounted Chasseurs, armed with the light cavalry sabre model An XI. The uniforms of this class of light horse were a fairly sombre green differenced only by regimental facing colours and other small details. Apparently the 1806 pattern shako was not popular, replacing as it did various more colourful headgear; and after its reluctant adoption "tribal" differences often appeared at regimental level.